IntimateGardens

By C. Colston Burrell
with
Lucy Hardiman

Janet Marinelli
SERIES EDITOR

Sigrun Wolff Saphire
SENIOR EDITOR

Mark Tebbitt
SCIENCE EDITOR

Leah Kalotay
ART DIRECTOR

Joni Blackburn
COPY EDITOR

Steven Clemants
VICE-PRESIDENT,
SCIENCE &
PUBLICATIONS

Judith D. Zuk
PRESIDENT

Elizabeth Scholtz
DIRECTOR
EMERITUS

Handbook #180

Copyright © 2005 by Brooklyn Botanic Garden, Inc.

All-Region Guides, formerly *21st-Century Gardening Series*, are published three times a year at 1000 Washington Ave., Brooklyn, NY 11225.

Subscription included in Brooklyn Botanic Garden subscriber membership dues ($35 per year; $45 outside the United States).

ISBN # 1-889538-65-5

Printed by Science Press, a division of the Mack Printing Group. Printed on recycled paper.

A beautifully designed and planted garden room draws everyone out of the house, inviting adults and children to relax, play, and explore the natural world.

Intimate Gardens

Intimate Gardens

Most people who are setting out to create a garden for a new house, or to revitalize an existing property, face the challenge of making their paradise in a relatively small space. As our property boundaries shrink and our lives become more frenzied, our gardens have become havens from the hectic, crowded world. Even those blessed with larger properties want to create intimate outdoor spaces. Rather than an uncomfortable view of the neighbors' living room or kitchen, we want a sense of privacy and enclosure. We also long for a stronger connection with the natural world, and find it in the garden. We definitely want a place to entertain or relax outdoors, and gardens that function as outdoor rooms answer that call as well.

For decades, typical American gardens were anything but intimate. They followed the dictates of Andrew Jackson Downing, the 19th century's arbiter of taste and author of the influential 1841 publication *A Treatise on the Theory and Practice of Landscape Gardening, Adapted to North America*. Downing's landscapes were open and expansive and his houses were surrounded with vast greenswards. He equated the presence of a lawn with good taste when he wrote, "Already the finer places on the Hudson and about Boston boast many finely kept lawns, and we hope ... to see this indispensable feature ... becoming ... more universal." Though Downing promoted segregating various activities in different outdoor areas, including dividing

Left: With its axial layout, this garden draws on the tradition of symmetrical formal designs. Perfectly in scale with the building, the evergreen boxwood pillars lead the way to the entrance, flanked on both sides with small garden rooms. The footed urn sets a playful accent that echoes the rounded arch of the doorway.

spaces into ornamental and service areas, the convention of open spaces with expansive lawns long remained the norm.

The current desire for intimate gardens is nothing new, however. Intimacy, comfort, and a connection with nature have long been important considerations for garden makers. The earliest pleasure gardens were enclosed, cloistered spaces. Walls surrounded the Persian gardens of the 1st century. They shut out the world, including the harsh climate of the Middle East, where they were built. These garden walls surrounded square or rectangular spaces that followed a tradition of symmetry. At the heart of the garden was a fountain, usually circular, square, or octagonal, which represented the universe. From the central fountain flowed four rills, or streams, representing the four rivers of life. Symbolically, water, wine, milk, and honey flowed from the center of the universe. The rivers divided the garden into quadrants. This geometry dominates formal design to this day.

Cottage gardens, which first appeared in 15th-century England, were quite another type of early garden room. They were usually bordered by a fence or a hedge meant to keep out marauding livestock. Cottage gardens were a pastiche of plantings, often with an informal seating area sequestered somewhere within. Originally they featured

all the plants that a household would require for cooking, as well as for medicinal and other practical uses. In time, they became mainly ornamental; they framed the view of the house and enlivened the approach to the front door, blurring the lines between indoors and out.

Victorian garden enthusiasts were enamored of the plants coming into England and America from all around the

An informal planting of herbaceous plants and small trees shelters the porch and sends a warm welcome to anyone approaching it. Allowing views in and out, the plantings create a comfortably enclosed space and an appealing transition between inside and outside.

Open invitations to linger and appreciate the garden, places to sit are all-important garden features. Backed by an informal planting of tall evergreens that has mellowed over time, the weathered seat is a place for a quiet retreat. A larger terrace, just visible on the right, is a welcoming place for gatherings.

world. They commonly displayed these exotic species in lush plantings around a well-defined open space intended to give order to the flowery tumble. Victorians had an intimate relationship with their gardens. They used their lawns like outdoor rooms— for relaxation, theatrical productions, and games. The garden was also a place for a stroll, to get fresh air and a bit of exercise, with beds of colorful plants as a backdrop. The garden was a destination to be visited before returning to the comfort of a terrace or gazebo near the house.

Harmony of form, style, and function was artfully realized in the Arts and Crafts movement that influenced English and American architecture and landscape gardening in the early 20th century. This style melded house and garden in a way that until then had been largely unexplored on a small scale. Plantings were used to accent the lines of the house and to emulate the beauty of nature that had been driven ever further from people's everyday lives since the beginning of the industrial revolution. Garden spaces were directly related to the house, often sharing the same construction materials, especially wood and stone. Pergolas and similar structures were often used to blur the distinction between indoors and outdoors.

The Prairie style, a version of the Arts and Crafts style from the American Midwest, was promoted by such influential architects as Louis Henri Sullivan, William Gray Purcell, and Frank Lloyd Wright. Prairie-style houses had long horizontal lines, reflecting the wide horizon so visible in the prairie landscapes of the region. The garden, too, was inspired by the natural landscape. Native prairie was re-created, and shrubs and trees were used en masse to draw out the lines of the architecture and marry the house to the garden.

In the 1940s and 1950s, prominent American landscape architects such as Garrett Eckbo and Thomas Church began promoting a new philosophy of landscape architecture that challenged established conventions and eschewed design tenets based on the English landscape and Arts and Crafts styles that had emerged in the 1920s and 1930s. The focus of the modernist landscape designers turned from the garden as a horticultural showplace to the garden as a space for socializing.

In his 1955 manifesto, *Gardens Are for People,* Church wrote, "Even the term garden has changed its meaning. A garden used to have a horticultural meaning. It was

Designed for outdoor living, this deck is a wonderful spot for a meal. Keeping the harsh afternoon sun at bay, the leafy tree cover creates mellow dappled light that eases the transition between indoors and out. Potted shrubs add a touch of color and fragrance and break up and soften the horizontal lines of the railing.

The experience of this small garden nook is enriched by the small pond, which reflects its surroundings and adds a little bit of movement to an otherwise still environment.

a place to walk through, to sit in briefly while you contemplated the wonders of nature before you returned to the civilized safety of indoors. The new kind of garden … is designed primarily for living, as an adjunct to the functions of the house. How well it provides for the many types of living that can be carried on outdoors is the new standard by which we judge a garden." These new outdoor spaces had an open, expansive aesthetic, surprisingly similar to what Downing had promoted a century earlier, but based on a more active outdoor lifestyle and scaled down from an expansive estate to the size of an average suburban lot.

Church believed that "people want their gardens to provide many pleasures, conveniences, and comforts; none but dyed-in-the-wool gardeners want them to be any work." Americans took him to heart, and the garden was viewed merely as a backdrop for casual recreation and elegant entertaining.

The meaning of the garden is changing once again. We still want beautiful outdoor rooms for socializing. But we want our gardens to be more than backdrops for barbecues or cocktail parties. Today, the ideal garden is also a place of refuge, where plants not only define spaces and provide privacy but also promote a sense of wonder and intimate involvement in the day-to-day drama of nature. This handbook shows how to create such a captivating outdoor space.

Designing an Intimate Garden

An intimate garden is more than a seat or terrace surrounded by greenery. Intimacy comes when a variety of elements coalesce into a harmonious composition. These elements include well-proportioned spaces, a comfortable sense of enclosure, and captivating plants. Perhaps most important is your relationship with these elements, because no garden, no matter how well designed, will feel intimate if you are not involved in the day-to-day rhythms that take place, whether shifting shadow patterns cast by trees or shrubs throughout the day, or the changing of the seasons—from the unfolding of flowers to the ripening of fruits and the turning of leaves.

Getting Started

The easiest way to start designing an intimate garden is to address your practical needs first. One of the most important considerations is deciding where you want to put sitting areas and gathering spaces, which are the heart and soul of the intimate garden. Consider the possibilities: a breakfast terrace located to catch the warm morning sun, an afternoon reading nook tucked under a leafy canopy. On a patio or deck close to the house, surrounded with fragrant and luminous plants, can be the perfect place for a relaxing evening meal. Sketching out such practical spaces can help

Left: Sketching out the most desirable places for sitting areas and gathering spaces—as well as the way to get to them—can help you determine how best to configure the garden and what trees, shrubs, and herbaceous plants to choose.

Circular shapes, such as this lawn, can be soothing, as they avoid hard edges and give equal importance to every spot along the perimeter. A small lawn does double duty as a play area and a space for occasional large gatherings.

you determine the configuration of the planting areas and the types of plants that are most appropriate. So, before you start placing island beds and picking perennials, decide where terraces, benches, and other functional elements will go, how much space they'll take, and how you will reach them.

Begin with a map of your yard, including the walls of the house and any existing permanent features such as walkways and trees. Use trace-paper overlays to draw potential shapes, and explore possible placements. Experiment with round, rectilinear, or curving forms of various sizes until you find a configuration that looks right. Next, using a can of marking paint and a tape measure, spray the lines of the space on the ground. (Don't worry: The grass will not be killed and will soon grow long enough that you can mow off the paint.) Once you've sprayed the space, look at it from all possible vantage points. Put a table and chairs or a bench in it to make sure it's the correct size. It's a lot easier to change the size of a painted space than one that has been built, so do your experimenting now!

MARRYING HOUSE AND GARDEN

Outdoor rooms are essentially extensions of our homes, so they should be related to the style, scale, and design of the house. There are many different ways in which a garden can reflect your home's architecture. A traditional dooryard garden in a four-square design would complement an old colonial farmhouse. A symmetrical house with two identical wings would call for a formal, symmetrical garden design, perhaps with an axial layout. A lush planting of old-fashioned flowers around a well-defined space to give order to the informal exuberance would suit a Victorian cottage. A bungalow garden could have straight lines but very informal, asymmetrical plantings. A ranch house with its door placed off center in the facade could be enhanced by an equally asymmetrical garden layout, perhaps with the terrace aligned with the long portion of the facade and low plantings framing the short side.

Whatever style you choose, stick with it. If you have a large garden and you want to change styles to add interest, you can divide it into several smaller, more intimate rooms, but be sure to design the transitions carefully to avoid a piecemeal look (see "Creating Intimacy in a Large Garden," page 22).

SHAPE

To create a sense of intimacy, design terraces, planting beds, or lawn areas as rectangular, circular, or curvilinear spaces, but avoid squiggly curves. Rectangular forms blend well with all architectural styles. They are often the best choice for small spaces because they lack ambiguity: The space is easy to understand as the eye moves along the borders without interruption. What's more, the crisp, uninterrupted lines can make a

As the round pool in this small garden focuses attention inward, it creates intimacy on a small scale. To draw attention outward, the wall has been painted a striking color, with a display of art adding more interest.

Rectangular shapes blend well with all architectural styles. They are often a good choice for small gardens as they avoid ambiguity: The space is easy to understand as the eyes move easily along the lines without interruption. For a longer view of this garden, see the photo on the facing page.

space seem larger. Rectangular spaces also reflect the shape of most indoor rooms, which adds to the feelings of familiarity and comfort.

Circular spaces, which create an inward focus, can also be intimate. A round garden space is very effective at the end of a visual axis such as a straight path or allée, or placed along a trail where it can be encountered spontaneously while traveling through the garden. Jens Jensen, who pioneered the Prairie style in garden design, believed that a circle gives "order to the randomness of nature." He also thought of the circle as a democratic form that placed everyone equidistant from the center. Jensen used circular "council rings" in all his gardens to achieve a great sense of intimacy.

Sinuous, sweeping curves are especially popular today—they denote a comfortable informality that appeals to many contemporary gardeners. It's worth noting, though, that curves usually work best in large spaces. A space with many curves loses its integrity because there is no well-defined edge. Picture a living room with curving walls of different shapes and different lengths, and you can imagine how curving lines might detract from a sense of comfort in an outdoor room.

SCALE AND PROPORTION

Proper scale and proportion, which govern the overall size and shape of an outdoor room, have a major impact on the intimacy of a garden. Your overriding concern should be to create an outdoor room that is in balance with the scale or mass of the house, existing trees, and other elements with which it is connected.

Scale is the relative size of a space or element in relation to the context in which it is placed. Think of a vase on a table and how you can easily see if it is too large or too small for the table. The same relationship exists outdoors. In a small garden, a space that is too large consumes the property and leaves no room for plantings or other forms of enclosure; and without enclosure, there is no feeling of intimacy. Conversely, in a sea of lawn, a small bench becomes lost and looks as awkward and uninviting as a tiny area rug in a large living room—the scale is all wrong.

Proportion is the ratio of one dimension to another, such as width to length. The ancient Greeks and Romans developed a highly refined sense of proportion, evident in both the architecture and gardens of the ancient world. They used the rule of proportion known as the Golden Mean, which is represented by the ratio 1 to 1.618. You can easily use classical proportions when laying out your garden: simply multiply the short dimension of the proposed space by 1.618 to determine what the longer dimension should be. In other words, a terrace that is 13 feet wide should be approximately 21 feet long. A quick way to think of this proportion is to use the general rule of thirds. A space should be two thirds longer than it is wide, for example. For a quick look at a shape based on the Golden Mean, get out your credit card, and there it is.

You can manipulate the feeling of intimacy in a garden with the placement of objects. Place a focal point like a bench one third of the way from the viewing point for an intimate feel. For a more expansive impression, accentuate the perspective by placing the bench two thirds of the way into the space from the viewing point.

Finding just the right scale and proportion is vital for creating a sense of intimacy in a garden. This outdoor room, a longer view of the garden pictured on the left, is in balance with the building, trees, and other elements with which it is connected.

For example, place your bench in a grove of trees, perhaps with shrubs for added enclosure, to give it some context. The bench becomes a destination, and the experience of sitting on the bench is more sensual amid the greenery.

Enclosing Spaces

Enclosure is the key to creating intimacy in any garden, no matter the scale. Enclosed does not necessarily mean walled off, however. Different circumstances require different degrees of enclosure. Vary the height and density of the wall or screen according to your needs. The side of your house, stone walls or fences, hedges, pergolas, or even strategically placed potted plants can all be used to create a sense of enclosure.

THE WALLS OF YOUR HOUSE

An outdoor room adjacent to your house in effect already has one solid wall. It is easiest to create an outdoor room that is in scale with a single-story house. If you have a taller one, you may need to take some steps so the house appears more in scale with an intimate garden room. Try covering the wall with a trellis to create a green screen.

To break up a blank expanse, you can display a piece of art or paint a mural. Place a mirror on the wall to make a tiny patio or deck feel larger. If the wall is too overpowering for the space, consider planting a tree or two to separate the space from the house. The trees will form a smaller green "wall" that also provides an intimate ceiling of leafy branches over your outdoor room.

As extensions of our homes, gardens should be related to the style and scale of the house. In this Prairie-style planting, the garden also takes its cue from the surrounding landscape, which is rather flat with occasional vertical relief.

In addition to marking boundaries and blocking unattractive views, architectural elements like walls and fences can be used to create a sense of intimacy in an outdoor room. Allowing the movement of sound, air, and light through its window openings, this wall captures the drama of the outdoors as it shelters the garden.

GARDEN WALLS, FENCES, AND TRELLISES

Most homeowners think of garden walls and fences, including trellises, when they want to mark boundaries or block unattractive views. These architectural elements can also be used to create a sense of intimacy in an outdoor room. An added benefit is that a wall or fence can double the gardening space in a small area, because it offers the opportunity of gardening vertically with beautiful flowering vines and hanging containers. (See the list of flowering vines on page 110.)

Where you want to define space without blocking views, low garden walls are very effective. By surrounding an open space with a low wall that's comfortable for sitting, you define the borders of the space, make it more intimate, and have a pleasant place to sit as well. On sloping ground, a wall can also be used to create a dramatic grade change, which not only offers enclosure but also may be less work in the long run than maintaining a hillside planting.

HEDGES

Hedges can fulfill the same functions as walls and fences; which to choose is a matter of context and taste. If space is at a premium, use a fence or planted trellis. Where space is more ample, use a hedge. Clipped boxwood hedges are the traditional

Paving Materials

Terraces, decks, and other paved surfaces are part of the garden's floor. Choose materials to match or compliment those of the house and other garden architecture. City gardeners may want to consider using concrete, to reflect the urban infrastructure. Colonial houses traditionally have brick paths. Stone, gravel, mulch, and grass are other materials commonly employed for paths. Whatever material you choose, carry the theme through, changing only when the grade changes or when you pass from one room to the next.

CONCRETE: Poured concrete can be pressed, dyed, or decorated with stone inlay. California, in particular, has a plethora of recycled concrete available to gardeners, no doubt due to the aftermath of earthquakes. This concrete material can be used as random pavers or cut to make regular pavers; it can even be used to build walls. Various modular brick or Belgian block shapes with textured surfaces are widely available, often dyed in brick or earth tones. And due to their modular, often interlocking nature, they are easy to lay, structurally sound, and hard wearing.

BRICK: Brick is a tried-and-true material that can add either casual elegance or formality to a space, depending on the density and color of the brick and the paving pattern. Favored since colonial times, brick is common around historic homes and remains a popular material, especially in the South. Brick can be laid wide side down (bedding face), or narrow side down (stretcher face) in a variety of patterns, including running bond, herringbone, and basket weave.

STONE AND GRAVEL: Nothing conveys a sense of place like native stone. Stones can be used in their natural shapes or cut into square or rectangular patterns. They can be laid in random, patchwork, or modular designs. Gravel is an inexpensive and easy-to-install alternative to large stone, which must be skillfully laid.

PEBBLES: Pebbles and pebble mosaics were once popular in gardens, in part because the materials and labor were cheap. Today, the materials remain inexpensive, but the labor costs are not. However, many exquisite pebble and tile mosaics are still being created by artisans and make lovely surfaces in a garden room or along a path.

WOOD: Decks are popular alternatives to hard elements, but they are not permanent. The average deck has a 20-year life expectancy. Use your imagination to create interesting patterns. Vary the width of the boards, run boards at right angles, or even consider diagonal placement to keep the surface interesting.

Where space allows, hedges are wonderful enclosures for intimate spaces. An informal border of mixed flowering shrubs or a more formal shaped hedge, as shown here, gently embraces the garden as it mellows over time.

choice for formal gardens, while untrimmed flowering shrubs create an informal wall. Openings in hedges that allow for views without providing physical access are another nice touch, creating a feeling of enclosure that's not too forbidding and invites peeking. Like a window in a wall, they allow you to see in or out. Hedges are also perfect backdrops for flower borders filled to overflowing with annuals and perennials.

ARBORS AND PERGOLAS

Arbors and pergolas can ease the transition from indoors to outdoors and extend a sense of privacy. They are especially effective at screening views from above and can be used instead of trees for this purpose. They create a porous ceiling, but you can make it more solid by covering it with vines or by combining it with trees. Try growing an open-crowned tree like sweetbay magnolia (*Magnolia virginiana*) up through the roof of a pergola for dramatic impact and maximum contrast between built and planted elements.

Intimacy can be achieved by re-creating layers found in natural plant communities. Taller trees screen the infinite space of the sky; smaller understory trees create a ceiling on a human scale; shrubs form appealing enclosing walls; and herbaceous plants provide visual interest at ground level.

Green Architecture

Another way to achieve intimacy in a garden setting is look to nature as a model, re-creating the vertical layers found in natural plant communities. A forest, for example, has a canopy formed by the tallest trees, an understory comprised of smaller trees, a shrub layer, and a ground layer of ferns, wildflowers, and mosses. The higher branches of trees can form the ceiling of an outdoor room. A ceiling provides shelter and visually screens the infinite realm of the sky. It is certainly possible, and sometimes desirable, to create intimacy outdoors with no ceiling—see the plan for a sunny courtyard garden on page 34, for example—but often the ceiling really defines the enclosure and sets the mood. Think of the way you feel in a concert hall versus the way you feel in your living room. The more intimate and comfortable feel of a living room is due to its more human scale. In the same way, small to midsize trees can be used to manipulate the scale of a space. Intimate spaces employ understory trees to create a low canopy that shelters and encloses.

continues on page 24

Left: Arbors and pergolas are effective at screening views from above and can be used instead of trees for this purpose. Here the arbor creates a lightweight ceiling in a garden room bounded by stone walls; it is made more attractive with a clematis vine that has started winding its way around the pillar.

Creating Intimacy in a Large Garden

A space does not have to be tiny to be intimate, but creating intimate gardens can be a challenge on large suburban lots or rural properties with big, undifferentiated spaces and expansive views. From a physical and psychological perspective, it is difficult to feel enfolded, cozy, and secure in such spaces. To feel comfortable, outdoor rooms should be designed on a human scale.

A good way to establish an intimate feeling in a large garden is to create a series of connected or interconnected spaces, or rooms, much as if they were a series of individual rooms in a house. Just as you might walk indoors from the kitchen to the dining room, and from there down the hall, you can travel through a series of varying but connected outdoor spaces.

Arrange a sequence of garden rooms in a way that makes visual sense to anyone visiting the garden. Strollers need to understand the logic of the design in order to feel at ease and enjoy the voyage. Let the layout of your house give you cues as to where to position garden spaces and how to combine them. Doors and windows are your portals to the outdoors. When you look out a window into the garden, it should be appealing from that vantage point. This is especially meaningful from heavily visited rooms such as the kitchen and dining room. When you move out into the garden, your path should be attractive yet efficient. From a design perspective, it is also important that the garden relate back to the house, whether it is near or at a distance.

One of the nicest things to do in an intimate garden is eat. Dining areas should be close to the house to keep travel time to a minimum and encourage frequent use. In a large garden, you can easily dedicate several areas for eating, perhaps customizing a small patio near the kitchen for breakfast and situating another garden room where there's a view of the sunset during dinner. To avoid a cluttered look, be sure to screen sitting areas from each other, partially or completely.

Use hedges, walls, fences, or combinations of them to separate various garden spaces. Where appropriate, consider connecting spaces visually. Openings in hedges let you peek into other areas of the garden. A low hedge, flower border, or sitting wall defines garden spaces and allows viewing from one area to the next. In other cases, the space may be completely sequestered from the others, even separated by gates for utter privacy.

Pathways and other corridors guide travel through the garden. A straight path allows efficient travel through space and provides direct access. A meandering path stretches out the journey and may add interest by hiding and then revealing views, while at the same time making travel more intimate.

A low retaining wall frames the entrance to the garden area at the top of the stairs, which is partially blocked from view by perennials and shrubs. As visitors walk up the steps to get a better look, they enter deeper into the garden, drawn by the mystery of the journey ahead.

Another appealing way to scale down a large garden is to position small spaces at points along the route by which you like to explore your property. A walking tour may take you from the lawn through a meadow, along a stream, past a rock outcropping to a pond. Place your intimate gardens to take advantage of these natural features.

Partial enclosure of the garden can actually enhance your enjoyment of an expansive view. Compare it to the way in which we instinctively head for a table in a restaurant that allows us to sit with our backs to the wall and a view of the action. Keep this innate trait in mind when designing a comfortable, cloistered space in a larger garden. You can feel safe and at ease on a bench or terrace partially enclosed with walls or hedges and also have the view that a large garden provides.

Trees and shrubs, the ceiling and walls of an outdoor room, are key to creating enclosure and intimacy. Visually, shrubs give spaces a human scale, which makes them ideal for dividing the garden into several smaller areas.

Continued from page 21

Think of shrubs as the walls in outdoor rooms, reaching from 3 to 15 feet tall. Like hedges and fences, shrubs can screen unattractive views, divide the garden into rooms, create privacy, and provide a backdrop for a flower garden. Visually, they create spaces on a human scale.

Shrubs are essential garden elements for a variety of reasons: the breaking buds of deciduous shrubs often offer the first sign of spring in the late-winter garden; as the first flowers unfurl, life renews itself. Foliage soon follows, providing a myriad of textures to carry the garden through the dog days of summer. In the fall, deciduous shrubs herald the passing of the growing season with a blaze of yellows, reds, and oranges. Their bare branches stand as testimonial to their enduring nature as snow starts to collect along them. Evergreen shrubs add special interest to the garden during the dead of winter. Their foliage provides color; snow gathers on coniferous bows; and curled rhododendron leaves tell us when the mercury has dipped below freezing. These day-to-day changes in the garden's green architecture reinforce the intimate relationship between you and your garden.

Trees and shrubs, the ceiling and walls of an outdoor room, are most important in creating enclosure and intimacy, but the floor of the garden is where avid gardeners often have the most fun. Groundcovers, perennials, annuals, bulbs, and mosses make up the garden's ground layer, or carpet. This can be the most dynamic part of the garden but also the most labor-intensive. Perennial borders, for example need a lot of attention. A simple groundcover planting, perhaps with bulbs for spring interest, provides a lush look and is a lower-maintenance alternative that may be better suited to your lifestyle. (See page 108 and 112 for recommended perennials and groundcovers for your intimate garden.)

Defining Planting Areas

Once you have sketched out comfortable spaces, you can turn your attention to the particulars of the planting areas. This is a good time to go back inside and take a look at your planned garden from a window to consider views from the house. Do you want to see directly into the space, or will a veil of trees make it more enticing? Perhaps you want to be totally shielded from the house, so that coming upon the garden space on a stroll will create a sense of surprise. Open-crowned trees such as serviceberries (*Amelanchier*) and Japanese maple (*Acer palmatum*) are diaphanous, while

evergreens like pines (*Pinus*), and trees with dense crowns like redbuds (*Cercis*) will create a screen. Most shrubs will effectively block your view by creating green walls. Keep in mind that larger, wider plants require deeper beds, and upright or conical selections, such as yews (*Taxus*) and boxwoods (*Buxus*), can fit into narrow spaces.

Make sure you have access to all areas of the garden from the edges or from internal paths: The average

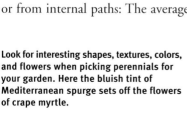

Look for interesting shapes, textures, colors, and flowers when picking perennials for your garden. Here the bluish tint of Mediterranean spurge sets off the flowers of crape myrtle.

Plants with great architecture such as this weathered Harry Lauder's walking stick are the cornerstones of a compelling design. It's also whimsical, and mood is as important as structure.

person can reach about two and a half feet into a planting bed, which means that beds accessible from two sides can be five to six feet deep without a central path; a border that's accessible from one side can be three feet deep, any wider and it will need a rear or central path.

CHOOSING PLANTS WITH PRESENCE

Once you've blocked out the most important practical spaces and planting areas in the garden, it's time to choose just the right shrubs and trees. Plants with great architecture—interesting and varied foliage shapes and textures, combined with good branching structure—are the cornerstones of a compelling design and should be top priorities. Beautiful inflorescences are a wonderful bonus, but as flowers are fleeting, it's the strong architectural plants that give structure to the garden and carry it through the seasons.

When choosing plants for your intimate garden, consider the sizes and forms of the trees and shrubs. In small gardens, proper plant choice is critical, and every plant must be carefully chosen to accomplish the dual goals of beauty and utility. Specimen plants and focal points should be dramatic, with exceptional branching or strong vertical form, so select highly architectural plants with good bones, or structure.

The plants in an intimate garden not only create a sense of structure and enclosure but also are critical in creating the proper mood. Choose plants that change with the seasons with flowers, fruits, or colorful autumn foliage. The more attractions a plant offers, the more involved you will be with that plant, leading to a more intimate relationship with your garden. Will the fragrance of an evening-flowering plant

Right: A generously meandering path partially hidden from view invites curious visitors to take a walk through the garden. The sheared shrubs and containers help direct strollers down the path.

The interplay between light and plants is one of the most enchanting and elusive aspects of a garden. As the angle and intensity of sunlight changes throughout the day, the way it mingles with leaves and stems is transformed, creating subtle or dramatic variations in mood.

entice you outdoors at day's end? Will the sinuous silhouette of a shrub lead you outside on a crisp winter afternoon?

Intimacy demands practicality as well. Consider evergreen plants for screening unattractive views or giving privacy year-round. Extend your seasonal enjoyment of the garden by contrasting deciduous plants that have brilliant fall color with evergreens such as pines (*Pinus*) and cedars (*Cedrus* and *Juniperus*) for dramatic effect. Plant colorful flowers that bloom during the season in which you will appreciate them most. Similarly, if you use a space mostly in the evening, consider planting white or pale yellow flowers, especially fragrant ones.

PLAYING WITH LIGHT

The interplay between light and plants is one of the most enchanting aspects of a garden. The quality of sunlight changes throughout the day, and so does the way it mingles with leaves and stems. Position architectural plants where they can interact with the sun. Backlighting the twisted stems of Harry Lauder's walking stick (*Corylus avellana* 'Contorta'), for example, is an enchanting way to reveal its intriguing structure. A fine-textured plant, a feathery willow (*Salix*), for example, often disappears into the garden fabric in the flat light of midday, but with backlighting it really stands out.

Luminescent foliage surfaces should not be overlooked. Think of foliage in terms of paint finishes that you might use in your home. The reflective qualities of plant leaves are similar to high gloss, semigloss, and matte-finish paints: The smooth, shiny leaves of camellias are high gloss; the hairy leaves of witch alder (*Fothergilla*) have matte finishes. Filtered light reflecting off a glossy groundcover seems to sparkle as the rays of light filter through the trees. Yellow or white variegated foliage brightens up a shady spot and turns it into a focal point, whereas a solid green plant might be lost in the gloom. The play of light and shade is, of course, ephemeral and unpredictable. Perhaps that is what makes it so compelling.

EMPHASIZING FRAGRANCE

Fragrance is perhaps the most alluring aspect of the garden, so it is a shame that so few plants other than roses are chosen for their scented leaves or flowers. Humid summer air carries fragrance throughout the garden and into the house. Nighttime is often the most fragrant time in the garden, and scent wafting through an open window can draw you outside to enjoy your outdoor room in the evening. Some plants perfume the air; others reveal their scent only up close.

Place all fragrant plants where you are likely to spend the most time, and locate those that yield their scent only at close hand in a spot where they are most likely to be appreciated. Position a pot of scented perennials and annuals near a seating area or table. Sweetbay magnolia (*Magnolia virginiana*) and perennials such as garden phlox and 'Casa Blanca' lilies (*Lilium* 'Casa Blanca') are good candidates for the beds surrounding a dining table.

Place fragrant plants, such as sweet pepperbush 'Pink Spires', where you are likely to spend the most time, and plant those that yield their scent only at close hand in a spot where they are most likely to be appreciated.

INTIMATE GARDEN PLANS:
A Simple Formal Terrace Garden

Whether you're trying to create a feeling of intimacy on a large property or in a small yard, this plan has ideas that will work for you. The terrace garden provides an outdoor living space with a cozy, roomlike scale. It has the same proportions as the lawn area beyond but is smaller in size and feels more intimate. Trees and shrubs have been planted to create a sense of enclosure: The large, spreading branches of the 'Heritage' river birch and star magnolia form a comfortable "ceiling" overhead. Small shrubs such as 'Carol Mackie' Burkwood daphne and medium-size shrubs like witch-hazel and fragrant Koreanspice viburnum form the "walls" of the outdoor room, enhancing the sense of privacy. The shrubs also connect the leafy canopy to the ground plane both visually and structurally, making the space work as a coherent whole. Woodland wildflowers, bulbs, sedges, and ferns provide a textural smorgasbord that changes with the seasons. The bank of Adam's needle in the partly sunny corner of the garden, in the right foreground, shows how a plant with presence can add drama to a small garden room. Via the stone walkway in the foreground, left, the terrace garden connects with other parts of the landscape; in smaller yards, the garden, which offers a pleasant spot for outdoor dining, can be located right next to the house.

Trees and Shrubs Featured in This Garden

1 *Betula nigra* 'Heritage', 'Heritage' river birch
2 *Daphne* × *burkwoodii* 'Carol Mackie', 'Carol Mackie' Burkwood daphne
3 *Hamamelis virginiana*, common witch-hazel
4 *Ilex verticillata* 'Red Sprite', 'Red Sprite' winterberry
5 *Magnolia stellata*, star magnolia
6 *Viburnum carlesii*, Koreanspice viburnum
7 *Yucca filamentosa*, Adam's needle

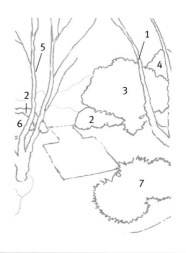

See the encyclopedia beginning on page 41 to choose plants appropriate for your climate and garden.

INTIMATE GARDEN PLANS:
A Shady Woodland Garden

This plan shows how to integrate an intimate garden into surrounding tall trees by using the existing "green architecture" to shelter the space and adding plants that enhance the sense of intimacy and provide year-round interest. Nestled at the base of a steep slope, the garden is crowned by native alders, big leaf maple, and Douglas fir on two sides and the house on a third (in the foreground, not shown). A stone wall on the fourth side embraces the circular seating area and supports the slope. Plants in the beds along the gently curving walkway guide visitors to the garden room. A vine-covered trellis and adjacent evergreen boxwood hedge mark the entry into the space. A witch-hazel anchors the far end, reaching up into the surrounding trees; later, its flowers offer much-appreciated late-winter color. Given the surrounding native woodland, the shade-loving plants that encircle the intimate living space need be no more than three to four feet tall, such as the Burkwood daphne. These shrubs and perennials have been chosen with an eye to year-round interest. The space feels like an enchanting clearing in the forest where you can bask on a chaise in the warmth of the sun.

Trees and Shrubs Featured in This Garden

1 *Buxus sempervirens*, common boxwood

2 *Camellia sasanqua*, autumn camellia

3 *Clethra* 'Rubie Spice', 'Rubie Spice' sweet pepperbush

4 *Daphne* × *burkwoodii*, Burkwood daphne

5 *Hamamelis* × *intermedia*, witch-hazel

6 *Hydrangea quercifolia*, oakleaf hydrangea

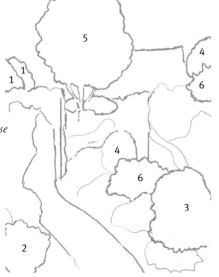

See the encyclopedia beginning on page 41 to choose plants appropriate for your climate and garden.

INTIMATE GARDEN PLANS:
A Sunny Courtyard Garden

You can create an intimate garden in the front yard as well as the backyard. This court-yard garden frames the front entry to a house, providing a pleasant spot to sit and an ele-gant transition point between the sidewalk, the front steps, and the back garden. The wall of the house anchors the courtyard, and the area has been raised up above ground level to help balance the building, giving the space a more human scale. The garden is in full sun, although surrounded by an array of trees and shrubs that not only create a sense of enclosure but also form a barrier that provides privacy from the street. In fact, the bench at the center of the space is invisible from the street in all seasons except win-ter, when the deciduous shrubs and small trees lose their leaves. The hinoki falsecypress is the pivotal plant in the design, forming an evergreen wall at the far end of the garden room, perpendicular to the house. If planted with evergreen perennials, the raised beds can furnish the garden with year-round color in shades of green, chartreuse, and silver.

Trees and Shrubs Featured in This Garden

1 *Acer palmatum*, Japanese maple
2 *Ceanothus thysiflorus* 'Skylark','Skylark' California lilac
3 *Chamaecyparis obtusa*, Hinoki falsecypress
4 *Cornus kousa*, Kousa dogwood
5 *Osmanthus* 'Goshiki', 'Goshiki' fragrant olive
6 *Vitex agnus-castus*, chaste tree

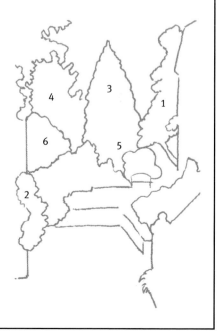

See the encyclopedia beginning on page 41 to choose plants appropriate for your climate and garden.

Furnishing an Intimate Garden

It takes more than a hammer and nails to make a home, and more than trees and shrubs, albeit beautiful ones, to make a garden. An intimate garden requires furniture and ornaments, the personal and perhaps even whimsical touches that make the garden uniquely yours.

Herbaceous Plants

Herbaceous perennials and groundcovers can be considered like living ornaments in the garden. Others make cameo appearances, then retreat into the background or disappear entirely for the remainder of the season. To keep your garden interesting, choose a combination of one-shot wonders like bulbs and spring ephemerals, as well as season-long beauties such as hostas and bears breeches (*Acanthus*). Annuals and tender perennials such as cannas provide color and texture through most of the growing season, too. Attractive seed heads, berries, and dried foliage will add to the show in winter.

The hues of flowers and foliage help set the mood of the garden. Purples, blues, and greens as well as pale pinks and pale yellows are known as cool colors. Cool-colored flowers seem to meld with their background. Visually, they soothe the eye. In contrast, the hot colors, such as bright yellows, oranges, reds, and deep magenta are

Left: Living ornaments, herbaceous plants such as tall colorful hollyhocks make an appearance at their allotted time, then retreat into the background for the remainder of the season.

visually very exciting: They seem to leap at you from the garden. Hot-color gardens are like a sultry breeze on a summer afternoon. They are riveting and sensual. Foliage color, whether green, red, yellow, or gray will also play a major role in creating your garden's ambience and entice you into the garden after the flowers are gone.

Garden Furniture

Tables, chairs, and benches, whether permanent or portable, are decorative as well as functional. A single chair is a piece of sculpture when not in use and a welcome place to sit and read or to admire the garden when it's needed. A bench placed at the end of a vista or allée stops the eye and helps to focus it on a spot that merits attention. A seat hidden behind a bend in a path adds the element of surprise. A dining ensemble creates a functional focal point in the garden.

Versatile Containers

Planted pots, urns, washtubs, and other vessels are decorative elements that not only expand the space for growing plants but also serve various other design purposes. Containers can be planted with annuals, bulbs, and perennials for a shifting seasonal

display or with an ornamental shrub or small tree for an elegant focal point. They can be dropped into a bed or spot in the garden wherever a bit of seasonal color or special drama is needed; when a spectacular plant finishes flowering or goes dormant, a carefully chosen potted specimen can easily carry the spot for the remainder of the growing season. Containers made of concrete, iron, lead, and plastic offer year-round durability outdoors.

Sending a warm welcome, the potted rose is a lovely focal point that sets the tone for the entrance area.

Whether smooth, as in this pond, trickling, spouting, or cascading, water is universally appealing. To make a major statement, water features don't have to be large: Waterproof containers such as iron kettles, urns, and glazed pots make wonderful water gardens—they also attract thirsty birds and other wildlife.

Water Features

Water adds a unique dimension to the garden. It reflects the warmth of the sun and the world around it, and brings the color of the sky and the patterns of clouds to earth. It also adds an audible dimension as it trickles, spouts, or cascades from a fountain or other water feature. Water features can be placed as focal points in beds and borders, on a terrace or deck, or wherever else you need to make a major statement.

Iron kettles, urns, and glazed pots all make great containers for small water gardens. Try a simple basin, floating glass balls in still water, or add a bubbler. You can also fill a pot with decorative water plants like sweet flag (*Acorus calamus*) and zebra rush (*Scirpus zebrinus*). A single lotus (*Nelumbo*) is enough to fill a glazed urn in a sunny spot.

Serious water gardeners will want more space than a container can offer. Basins, pools, and ponds create opportunities for gardening with aquatics on a larger scale. Floating plants like water-lilies (*Nymphaea*), emergents like pickerel weed (*Pontederia*), and bog plants such as elephant ears (*Alocasia*) and blue flag iris (*Iris versicolor*) lend a diversity of forms to the water garden.

Wildlife also benefits from water. Give birds a safe drinking place with water less than two inches deep. If your water basin or birdbath is deeper, place a brick in the center for birds to stand on, or place a potted water plant just below the surface.

After all the hard work of designing and installing your garden, it's time to accessorize it. All you need is a sense of fun and a little imagination: The possibilities for ornamentation are endless.

Playful Ornaments

In gardening, as in fashion, accessories make the ensemble. Many gardeners find ornamentation one of the hardest things to do. To accessorize your garden, all you need is a little imagination and a sense of adventure. Ornaments may be focal points or may be subtly woven into the garden fabric.

Traditional pieces such as statues, large vases, and sundials make a statement in a lawn or incorporated into a garden bed, and they also work well at the end of a vista or in the center of an open space. Urns, vases, and planters can combine plants and ornaments or stand alone. A single, unplanted container adds a dramatic focus to a bed of fine-textured plants.

Gazing balls made their debut as fancy Victorian trifles and have been drifting in and out of favor for a century. The wonder of gazing balls is that they offer the gardener unique vantage points. They mirror the garden, enabling you to see yourself within your garden. Resist the temptation to mount a gazing ball on a pedestal meant for a bird bath and banished to the center of a lawn. Instead, place one or more gazing balls within the heart of the garden room, surrounded by plants but easily viewed from a path or gathering space. Each time you pass, you can watch yourself move through the garden and see yourself reflected among your plants.

Architectural artifacts such as columns from old houses and discarded pavers make enchanting decorations. They link the past with the present. Utilitarian objects such as rakes can be reassigned new roles in the modern garden as trellises or plant stakes. The most vernacular ornaments can be charming in the right setting. Tractor seats, plows, old reel mowers, even rusted tractors can be incorporated to appealing effect. Even plaster gnomes, plastic geese, and plywood cutouts of gardeners' derrieres with lace knickers have a place for those who appreciate them. When it comes to accessorizing your garden, your own taste or sense of humor are the only constraints.

Encyclopedia of Plants for Intimate Gardens

This plant encyclopedia is divided into two main parts. From page 42 to page 75 you will find portraits of 30 evergreen and deciduous trees. From page 76 to page 107 you will find portraits of 30 evergreen and deciduous shrubs. In addition to the featured trees and shrubs, you will find lists of outstanding vines, herbaceous perennials, and groundcovers starting on page 108. All plants have been carefully chosen to provide for a wide range of forms, colors, and textures, and all excel in their dramatic presence.

To be in scale with the average urban or suburban garden, almost all the trees are small to medium in size, and many have attractive flowers, fruits, or bark. Shrubs have been chosen to provide year-round interest with appealing foliage, flowers, fruits, or bark. In intimate spaces every plant counts, so choose carefully, focusing on trees and shrubs that give the greatest impact and also fulfill your design goals. In addition to aesthetics, carefully consider the growing conditions in your area, matching the plants to the site's exposure, soil, and available moisture. Be sure to choose plants hardy in your area. For a map of USDA Plant Hardiness Zones, see page 114.

Trees

Acca sellowiana (Feijoa sellowiana) Pineapple Guava, Feijoa

Native Habitat and Range Woodland edges and clearings from Brazil to northern Argentina

Hardiness and Cultivated Range Zones 8 to 10; coastal areas from Virginia south to Florida, west to Texas, California, north to British Columbia

Landscape Form Pineapple guava is a small, often multistemmed tree, 15 to 20 feet tall and 10 feet wide.

Uses Tall screen, hedge if pruned or sheared

Ornamental Attributes This luscious evergreen grows as a large shrub to small tree with medium-textured leathery oval leaves that are green above and gray below. It has showy carmine flowers with deep red stamens and curled petals that are white on the undersides. Its edible, sweet-scented round fruits are abundant if cross-pollination occurs between different clones.

Tolerances Drought, salt, wind, moderate air pollution

Growing Tips Plant pineapple guava in average to humus-rich well-drained neutral to acidic soil in full sun or light shade. Fast growing and dense, it takes hard pruning. It is pest- and disease-free. Stems will be killed to the ground at 0°F; it can be grown as a dieback shrub in Zone 7.

Cultivars and Related Species Acca sellowiana 'Coolidge' fruits abundantly; 'Pineapple Gem' is a self-fertile selection.

Native Alternative Myrica cerifera, southern waxmyrtle, has a similar wide, rounded form, with linear, olive-green leaves. Though it lacks the showy flowers of pineapple guava, the fragrant gray-blue berries and evergreen foliage make it an admirable substitute. Found in coastal regions from Delaware to Florida and west to Texas (Zones 7 to 10), it grows well in average soil.

Acer palmatum | Japanese Maple

Native Habitat and Range Woodland edges and woodlands in China, Japan, Korea

Hardiness and Cultivated Range Zones 4 to 9; Nova Scotia, British Columbia,

Left: In midsummer, showy flowers enliven pineapple guava, which can serve as an effective evergreen year-round screen in mild climates.

Japanese maple cultivars are slow growing and come in many shapes and colors. Complementing the wooden structure in the back, this striking specimen adds an attractive touch of bronze to a garden of muted greens and gives height to an otherwise flat landscape.

south to Georgia, New Mexico, northern California

Landscape Form This upright, oval to rounded, small to midsize tree grows 15 to 30 feet tall and 10 to 25 feet wide and may be single-stemmed or clump forming. Cultivars vary in size, shape, foliage texture, and foliage color.

Uses Specimen tree, small shade tree, container plant

Ornamental Attributes This is a beautiful small tree with elegant branching and fine- to medium-textured palmate foliage that turns bright red in late autumn. It provides a fine- to medium-textured winter silhouette.

Tolerances Moderate drought, moderate air pollution, acidic soils

Growing Tips Plant Japanese maple in humus-rich neutral to acidic soil in full sun or partial shade. Its growth rate is moderate to slow and decreases with age: Depending on the cultivar, upright forms reach 15 to 20 feet in a decade. Foliage may brown in hot, dry weather. Plants may be susceptible to *Verticillium* wilt in wet years and in regions such as the Pacific Northwest. Some cultivars such as 'Bloodgood' can be invasive, especially in the Northeast. Check your state list before you plant.

Cultivars and Related Species *Acer palmatum* 'Bloodgood' is a popular cultivar with burgundy summer color; 'Sango-Kaku' is grown for its coral winter bark and fine-textured leaves; and *A. palmatum* Dissectum Atropurpureum Group has red summer foliage with threadlike segments. *A. griseum,* paperbark maple, is an upright tree to 35 feet with exfoliating chestnut bark and hairy leaves with three scalloped leaflets; it is native to China (Zones 5 to 8). The Japanese native *A. japonicum,* fullmoon maple (Zones 5 to 7), is an elegant, broad tree to 30 feet with round leaves of 9 to 11 incised lobes; 'Aconitifolium' is a popular cultivar with dramatically lobed leaves.

Native Alternative *Acer circinatum,* vine maple, is a small, rounded tree to 20 feet tall with an equal spread. The nearly round leaves are cut into seven broad lobes; it is native from British Columbia to California (Zones 5 to 7).

Amelanchier laevis
Allegheny Serviceberry

Native Habitat and Range Woodland edges, rock outcroppings, and roadsides from Nova Scotia to Ontario, south to Georgia, Iowa

Hardiness and Cultivated Range Zones 4 to 9; Nova Scotia, British Columbia, south to Georgia, New Mexico, northern California

Landscape Form This small- to midsize, upright oval or rounded tree grows 20 to 40 feet tall and 10 to 12 feet wide; it may be single-stemmed or clump forming.

Uses Specimen tree, shade tree, tall hedge if pruned or sheared

Ornamental Attributes Allegheny serviceberry has clustered white flowers in early spring and edible berries that ripen from red to dark blue in early summer. It has orange to red autumn color and silver to charcoal-gray bark.

Tolerances Moderate drought, moderate air pollution

Depending on your needs and preference, North American native Allegheny serviceberry can be trained to a single stem or grown as a clump with multiple slender stems.

Growing Tips Plant Allegheny serviceberry in average to humus-rich neutral to acidic soil in full sun or partial shade. Fast growing when young, it quickly reaches 15 to 20 feet; growth is moderate to slow with age. Plants may be susceptible to fire blight in some years and in some regions. Rust can be a problem, but many selections are resistant.

Cultivars and Related Species *Amelanchier arborea,* shadbush, is closely related but has downy new growth and leaves that emerge green rather than bronzy-red. *A. canadensis,* shadblow serviceberry, is a multistemmed clumpforming species that grows 10 to 20 feet tall and wide. *A. × grandiflora* 'Ballerina' is a compact plant to 20 feet tall with good autumn color; 'Cumulus' blooms profusely and has an upright oval form; 'Princess Diana' excels in color, and its fruits are large and sweet.

Betula nigra | River Birch

Native Habitat and Range Low woods, stream edges, and riverbanks in Massachusetts, southeastern Minnesota, south to northern Florida, eastern Texas

Hardiness and Cultivated Range Zones 4 to 9; Maine, British Columbia, south to Florida, New Mexico, northern California

Landscape Form River birch is an upright, oval, medium- to large-size tree, 40 to 60 (sometimes up to 75) feet tall and 20 to 30 feet wide; it may take a single-stemmed or clump form.

Uses Specimen tree, shade tree, tall hedge if pruned or sheared

Ornamental Attributes The exfoliating bark of a young river birch is cream- to peach-colored; the tree has fine-textured branches and medium-textured leaves with yellow fall color.

Tolerances Drought, soil compaction, flooding, moderate air pollution

Growing Tips Plant river birch in average to humus-rich acidic soil in full sun or partial shade. It is intolerant of alkaline soils. It grows fast when young and quickly reaches 30 to 40 feet but slows to moderate growth with age. It is short-lived—60 to 75 years. Though resistant to many pest and diseases that plague other birches, it has weak wood and may be damaged by ice.

Cultivars and Related Species *Betula nigra* 'Heritage' is a popular cultivar selected for heat tolerance and beautiful creamy-coral bark when young. *B. lenta,* black birch, is a drought-tolerant tree to 75 feet with wintergreen-scented twigs. A good birch for tough spots, though less ornamental except for excellent autumn color, it is native from Ontario to Alabama (Zones 3 to 7). The snowy-white bark of *B. papyrifera,* paperbark birch, which is native across northern North America from Zones 2 to 6, makes it a beautiful tree for northern regions. *B. occidentalis,* waterbirch, a similar, midsize tree to 60 feet with white bark, is native between the Rockies and the Cascades.

Cercidiphyllum japonicum
Katsura Tree

Native Habitat and Range Woodlands and forest edges in China, Japan

Hardiness and Cultivated Range Zones 5 (4 with protection) to 8; Nova Scotia, British Columbia, south to Georgia, New Mexico, northern California

Landscape Form The katsura tree takes a pyramidal to upright oval form in youth and grows rounded in old age. It is medium to large—40 to 60 feet tall and 20 to 30 feet wide. It may be single-

A fast grower when young, river birch can provide leafy cover for a garden room within a few years after planting.

This weeping form of the katsura tree has attractively arching branches. Whether cascading or upright and pyramidal, katsura tree's beautiful branching habit makes it a boon to small garden spaces in all seasons.

stemmed but usually grows in a clump form. It has medium-textured foliage and a fine-textured branching habit.

Uses Specimen, shade, or patio tree

Ornamental Attributes Graceful and upright, the katsura tree has pink-tinged spring foliage that expands to broad, heart-shaped gray-green leaves with scalloped edges. The foliage resembles redbud (*Cercis*), from which its botanical name derives. It has excellent yellow to apricot autumn color, and its winter silhouette is medium-textured and very decorative, especially in multistemmed clumps.

Tolerances Drought, moderate air pollution

Growing Tips Plant a katsura tree in average to humus-rich neutral to acidic soil in full sun or partial shade. It quickly reaches 15 to 20 feet tall, then slows in growth with age. Though it has no serious pests, it can be difficult and slow to establish: Transplant in early spring; balled and burlapped transplants suffer less shock than container-grown plants.

Cultivars and Related Species *Cercidiphyllum japonicum* 'Aureum' is decorative with purple new growth and bright yellow autumn color. 'Heronswood Globe' is a dwarf selection with a rounded form to 15 feet. *C. japonicum* f. *pendulum* is a gracefully weeping selection that ultimately reaches 25 feet tall by 30 feet wide, making a dramatic specimen plant.

Native Alternatives See *Cercis canadensis*, eastern redbud. It is a good alternative for the East and Midwest. In the West, choose *C. occidentalis* and in the Southwest, *C. reiniformis.*

Cercis canadensis | Eastern Redbud

Native Habitat and Range Open woodlands, forest edges, meadows, and roadsides from Pennsylvania to Nebraska, south to Florida, Texas

Hardiness and Cultivated Range Zones 4 to 8; Nova Scotia, British Columbia, south to Florida, the Gulf Coast, northern New Mexico, northern California

Landscape Form Eastern redbud is a wide, oval to round, small to midsize tree, 20 to 35 feet tall and 20 to 40 feet wide; it may take a single-stemmed or clump form.

Uses Specimen tree, patio tree, screen

Ornamental Attributes Rosy-purple flowers appear in dense clusters on bare branches in spring, followed by bold, heart-shaped gray-green leaves with yellow autumn color. Winter twigs have a medium-textured, attractive zigzag pattern.

Tolerances Drought, heat, alkaline and acidic soils, moderate flood, moderate air pollution

Growing Tips Plant eastern redbud in average to humus-rich soil in full sun or partial shade. It has a moderate growth rate when young, reaching 10 to 15 feet in a decade, with moderate to slow growth with age. It is a short-lived tree with an average lifespan of 30 to 50 years. It is very sensitive to salt and may be susceptible to canker.

Cultivars and Related Species *Cercis canadensis* f. *alba* is white-flowered; 'Appalachian Red' is bright pink; 'Covey' has a stiff trunk with weeping branches; 'Forest Pansy' has purple leaves that may fade to green where nights are warm. *C. canadensis* var. *texensis,* Texas redbud, has leathery deep green leaves and is extremely tough and drought tolerant. 'Oklahoma' is a densely flowered rosy magenta selection. *C. orbiculata,* California redbud, grows 20 to 30 feet tall and performs well on the West Coast, where other species are less successful. All are hardy in Zones 7 to 10.

Chamaecyparis obtusa | Hinoki Falsecypress

Native Habitat and Range Highland forests of Japan, Taiwan

Hardiness and Cultivated Range Zones 5 to 8; coastal New England to British

Eastern redbud, a midsize tree native to eastern North America, ushers in spring with a showy display of bright flowers.

Columbia, south to Georgia, New Mexico, California

Landscape Form Hinoki falsecypress is an upright, conical, mid- to large-size tree, 50 to 75 feet tall and 10 to 20 feet wide; compact selections are best for small garden rooms.

Uses Specimen tree, container plant, screen, tall hedge without pruning

Ornamental Attributes Hinoki falsecypress has lush, soft, deep green needles on fan-shaped branchlets that overlap like waves. The deep, moody color is perfect for a grotto or cozy corner, and the branches always invite stroking. Its erect form adds a dramatic vertical accent.

Tolerances Moderate drought, moderate air pollution

Growing Tips Plant Hinoki falsecypress in average to humus-rich well-drained neutral to acidic soil in full sun or partial shade and protect it from strong winds. It grows about 20 to 25 feet in 20 years.

Cultivars and Related Species *Chamaecyparis obtusa* 'Crippsii' has extended, frondlike branchlets of yellow needles where exposed to sun—the inner foliage is green. 'Nana Gracilis' is a dwarf, densely branching selection to six feet tall. Small cultivars of the Japanese native *C. pisifera,* sawara falsecypress, add lush evergreen foliage to the garden: 'Filifera Aurea' has golden, threadlike branchlets with small flat needles and slowly reaches 15 to 20 feet; 'Squarrosa' has blue needlelike leaves on dense plants that slowly reach 30 to 40 feet. All are hardy in Zones 4 to 8.

Native Alternative *Chamaecyparis nootkatensis,* Nootka falsecypress or Alaska cedar, forms a towering, weeping pyramid 20 to 50 feet tall (up to 100 feet in the wild). It is native to the Pacific Northwest (Zones 4 to 7).

Chilopsis linearis | Desert Willow

Native Habitat and Range Stream edges, arroyos, and riverbanks from central Texas west to southern California

Hardiness and Cultivated Range Zones 7 to 9; Virginia, Oregon, south to Florida, Arkansas, California

Landscape Form An upright, oval to round, small to midsize tree, 15 to 25 feet tall and 10 to 15 feet wide, desert willow may take a single-stemmed or clump form.

Uses Specimen tree, screen, tall hedge if left unpruned

Ornamental Attributes Desert willow's showy white and rose (occasionally pure

branching, open-crowned tree to 25 to 30 feet tall and wide. This hybrid does better in moist humid regions than the species.

Chionanthus virginicus
Fringetree, Old Man's Beard

Native Habitat and Range Woodland edges, rock outcroppings, and roadsides from New Jersey to Kentucky, Missouri, south to Florida, Texas

Hardiness and Cultivated Range Zones 4 to 9; Maine, British Columbia, south to Florida, New Mexico, northern California

Landscape Form Fringetree is an upright, oval to rounded, small to midsize tree, 20 to 35 feet tall and 10 to 20 feet wide; it may be low branching or form a clump.

Uses Specimen tree, patio tree (male clones are less messy in a small space), container plant, informal screen

Ornamental Attributes As its common names imply, this tree has large trusses of nodding, fragrant white flowers with thin, twisted petals like fringe. It has broadly lance-shaped, medium- to coarse-textured foliage with clear yellow autumn color. Fringetree is dioecious (having male and female flowers on separate plants); females produce copious amounts of blue-black berries.

Tolerances Moderate drought

Growing Tips Plant fringetree in humus-rich neutral to acidic soil in full sun (for best flowering) or partial shade. Transplant in spring. It has a moderate to slow growth rate when young, to 10 to 15 feet; growth slows with age. Fringetree is pest and disease resistant.

white) tubular flowers cluster at branch tips all summer. The linear, willowlike semievergreen to deciduous leaves have negligible autumn color, but the tree's thin, beanlike pods persist through winter, and its attractive, irregular to twisted form offers winter interest.

Tolerances Severe drought, extreme heat, high wind, air pollution, moderate salt

Growing Tips Plant desert willow in average sandy to humus-rich neutral to alkaline soil in full sun or light shade. It is intolerant of heavy, moist, or wet soil. When young it quickly reaches 10 to 15 feet; growth is moderate to slow with age.

Cultivars and Related Species *Chilopsis linearis* 'Burgundy' has deep magenta flowers; 'Marfa Lace' has semidouble, blush-pink flowers; 'Regal' is pale lavender with a magenta lip. An intergeneric cross with the much larger shade tree *Catalpa bignonioides,* called ×*Chitalpa tashkentensis* (Zones 6 to 9), offers large lavender flower clusters and broadly lance-shaped leaves on a usually multistemmed to low-

With its horizontal branches starting low and reaching far, fringetree can be put to good use as an open informal screen. The softly rounded shape of the tree easily embraces an open space, helping to create an enclosure on an intimate scale.

Cultivars and Related Species
Chionanthus retusus, Chinese fringetree (Zones 5 to 8), is an elegant tree with a more refined form and a broadly oval multistemmed crown 15 to 25 feet tall and wide. Plants have smaller flower clusters that mingle with the oval to elliptic, deep green lustrous leaves. The autumn foliage is yellow and the fruit dark blue-black. The bark is furrowed and may exfoliate on older trunks.

Cornus kousa | Kousa Dogwood, Chinese Dogwood

Native Habitat and Range Woodlands and forest edges in China, Japan, Korea

Hardiness and Cultivated Range Zones 5 to 8; coastal New England, southern Great Lakes region, British Columbia, south to Georgia, New Mexico, California

Landscape Form This upright, oval to rounded, small to midsize tree, 20 to 30 feet tall and 20 to 35 feet wide, may take a single-stemmed or clump form; it is often vase-shaped with arching branches.

Uses Specimen tree, patio tree

Ornamental Attributes Kousa dogwood has large, starry white flowers with four broad, pointed bracts surrounding a buttonlike cluster of small yellow flowers in late spring to early summer. In autumn, its elliptic dark green, medium-textured leaves with pointed tips turn glowing red and purple and hold for up to six weeks. The edible, red fall fruits look a little like globular raspberries. The bark of older trees is gray, taupe, and brown and may be exfoliating.

Tolerances Moderate drought, moderate air pollution

Growing Tips Plant kousa dogwood in

tibility to a number of diseases. 'Appalachian Spring' is an anthracnose-resistant cultivar.

Cotinus coggygria | Common Smoketree

Native Habitat and Range Woodland edges, clearings, and rock outcroppings of southern Europe east to China

Hardiness and Cultivated Range Zones 4 to 8; Nova Scotia, British Columbia, south to Georgia, New Mexico, California

Landscape Form An upright, oval to rounded, small tree 10 to 15 feet tall and wide, common smoketree takes a low-branching or clump form.

Uses Specimen tree, screen, hedge

Ornamental Attributes Smoketree has gray-green, paddlelike leaves that turn orange to red in autumn. Purple-leafed selections are particularly lovely. In summer, plumes of "smoke" billow from hairs on the stalks surrounding the insignificant flowers.

Tolerances Drought, alkaline soil, moderate air pollution

Growing Tips Plant common smoketree in average to humus-rich, well-drained soil in full sun or light shade. It is fast growing when young and quickly reaches ten feet; growth is fast to moderate with age. This plant can take severe pruning and is often cut back to the ground (coppiced) in late winter to promote straight, lush growth for maximum

full sun or partial shade in moist, well-drained acidic soil that is high in organic matter. Supplemental water is essential for the first few years after planting this fairly slow growing tree. Unlike the native species it is resistant to anthracnose; it may be susceptible to canker.

Cultivars and Related Species *Cornus kousa* 'Milky Way Select' produces a profusion of flowers; 'Satomi' ('Rosabella') has a rose-pink blush. The native *C. alternifolia,* pagoda dogwood (Zones 3 to 7), and Asian *C. controversa,* giant dogwood (Zones 5 to 7), grow 25 and 35 feet tall, respectively, with distinctive horizontal branches. Both have attractive variegated forms.

Native Alternatives *Cornus florida,* flowering dogwood, grows 20 to 30 feet tall and wide. A North American native (Zones 5 to 9), it remains a favorite spring-flowering tree despite its suscep-

Right: A striking focal point, this pink-flowering cultivar of common smoke tree grows into a small beautifully formed tree. For minimum bulk with maximum foliage and "smoke" impact, it can be cut back to the ground every year in late winter.

foliage impact with minimum bulk. Mature trees are beautifully formed and virtually pest free; they are susceptible to *Verticillium* wilt in the Northwest.

Cultivars and Related Species *Cotinus coggygria* 'Black Velvet' has deep purple leaves and thick "smoke"; 'Nordine' has red-violet foliage; 'Royal Purple' has red-violet new leaves that deepen to purple; 'Velvet Cloak' has deep purple leaves that retain their color even under high summer temperatures.

Native Alternatives Native to limestone regions of the lower Midwest (Zones 4 to 8), *Cotinus obovatus,* American smoketree, is a somewhat irregular to gnarly tree 30 feet tall, with large gray-green paddlelike leaves. Modest smoky plumes are borne in summer. 'Grace' is a purple-leafed hybrid resulting from a cross between the two species.

Cupressus arizonica; *C. arizonica* var. *glabra* | Arizona Cypress

Native Habitat and Range Woodland edges, clearings, and rock outcroppings from Texas west to Utah, California, south to central Mexico

Hardiness and Cultivated Range Zones 7 to 9; Virginia, Missouri, British Columbia, south to Georgia, Mexico, California

Landscape Form Arizona cypress is a conical to upright, oval evergreen tree, 40 to 60 feet tall and 25 to 30 feet wide.

Uses Specimen tree, screen, tall hedge

Ornamental Attributes This pyramidal, gray-blue conifer keeps beautiful form and fine texture in all seasons.

Thanks to its unusual foliage color and classically symmetrical pyramidal form, evergreen Arizona cypress attracts attention, drawing the eyes upward and emphasizing all vertical lines in the garden.

Tolerances Drought, heat, alkaline soil, moderate air pollution

Growing Tips Plant Arizona cypress in average to humus-rich, very well drained neutral soil in full sun. It grows at a moderate rate when young to 15 to 20 feet; growth is moderate to slow with age. Established plants are drought tolerant but can't take high humidity and heavy soil; they grow best in semi-arid to arid western regions. Under environmental stress, they may be susceptible to canker.

Cultivars and Related Species *Cupressus arizonica* 'Blue Ice' has blue-gray foliage, mahogany stems, and a strong conical form; 'Blue Pyramid' is gray-blue with an upright form; 'Limelight' has creamy lime-green to yellow foliage and a narrow conical form. *C. macrocarpa,* Monterey cypress, is a familiar sight along the California coast (Zones 7 to 9). This wind- and salt-tolerant conifer grows to 50 feet or more, with dramatic horizontal branches and an often

A midsize rounded tree for a moist, sunny to partly shaded location, two-winged silverbell welcomes spring with attractive white flowers. As the tree resents transplanting, it is important to carefully choose its home.

windswept form. America's most popular conifer for hedges and screening, ×*Cupressocyparis leylandii,* Leyland cypress (Zones 6 to 10), quickly grows to 20 or 30 feet (ultimately 60 to 70 feet tall), with rich green foliage and a feathery, upright form.

Halesia diptera var. *magniflora* Two-Winged Silverbell

Native Habitat and Range Moist woodland edges, streamsides, and swales in scattered locations from South Carolina to Tennessee, south to Florida, Texas

Hardiness and Cultivated Range Zones 5 to 9; Maine, Iowa, British Columbia, south to Florida, Texas, California

Landscape Form This oval to rounded, midsize tree is 20 to 40 feet tall and wide; it may be single-stemmed with low branches or take a clump form.

Uses Specimen tree, patio tree

Ornamental Attributes In spring, pendulous snow-white bells in clusters dangle from bare branches. The lush, broadly oval summer foliage turns yellow in autumn. The brown seedpods have two papery wings.

Tolerances Slight drought

Growing Tips Plant two-winged silverbell in moist, humus-rich neutral to acidic soil in full sun or partial shade. It has a moderate growth rate when young to 15 to 20 feet and slows with age. This pest-free tree doesn't transplant easily and is best planted in spring as containerized stock.

Cultivars and Related Species Native to woodlands from West Virginia and Illinois south to Florida and Oklahoma (Zones 5 to 8), *Halesia tetraptera* (syn. *H. carolina*), Carolina silverbell, is an elegant midsize (30 to 40 feet tall in cultivation) tree with smaller white flowers than its relations and striped bark and pointed, oval leaves. 'Rosea' has soft pink flowers; 'Variegata' has leaves edged in creamy yellow.

Hamamelis × *intermedia*
Witch-Hazel

Native Habitat and Range Offspring of two Asian parents, *Hamamelis mollis* from China and the Japanese native *Hamamelis japonica*

Hardiness and Cultivated Range Zones 5 to 8; Maine, Illinois, British Columbia, south to Georgia, New Mexico, northern California

Landscape Form Witch-hazel is a horizontally growing, oval, rounded, or spreading vase-shaped tree. It is small to midsize, growing 15 to 20 feet tall and wide, and it may take a multistemmed clump or low-branching form.

Uses Specimen tree, patio tree, pot plant

Ornamental Attributes Witch-hazels are the undisputed stars of the winter garden. Twisted, spiderlike fragrant flowers illuminate the landscape in vivid orange, sulfur to buttery-yellow, gold, and red. Broadly oval, scalloped leaves turn yellow to orange-red in autumn.

Tolerances Moderate drought, acidic soil

Growing Tips Plant witch-hazel in average to humus-rich, well-drained neutral to acidic soil in full sun to partial shade with protection from constant wind. It grows at a moderate rate when young to ten feet and more slowly with age. It has no serious pests, though Japanese beetles may munch the leaves.

Cultivars and Related Species *Hamamelis* × *intermedia* 'Arnold's Promise' has an upright vase shape and sunny yellow flowers in late winter; 'Diane' is an excellent red but has the annoying habit of holding its old foliage, which compromises the display; 'Jelena' has fragrant copper-orange blooms and incendiary fall color; 'Primavera' blooms early and has primrose-yellow flowers. *Hamamelis mollis,* Chinese witch-hazel, is vase-shaped with yellow flowers; 'Pallida' is a popular selection with early, soft yellow flowers.

Native Alternative *Hamamelis virginiana,* common witch-hazel, is an autumn-flowering species to 30 feet tall with a wide, vase-shaped form. It is native to moist woods from Nova Scotia and Wisconsin south to Florida and Texas (Zones 4 to 8). *Hamamelis vernalis,* Ozark witch-hazel, is an upright midwestern native that blooms in spring (Zones 4 to 8).

Plant witch-hazel in a spot where you can see it from inside the house. You don't want to miss the late-winter flowers of this lovely, vase-shaped small tree.

Provided their flowers get pollinated in spring, female specimens of yaupon, a small broadleaf evergreen holly, display large numbers of red berries from late summer through winter. The weeping cultivar 'Pendula' is used here to add panache to the entrance of a garden path.

Ilex vomitoria | Yaupon

Native Habitat and Range Low woodland edges, fields, and marshy spots from coastal Virginia west to Missouri, south to Florida, Texas

Hardiness and Cultivated Range Zones 7 to 10; coastal Massachusetts, eastern Pennsylvania, west to Missouri, coastal British Columbia, south to Florida, California

Landscape Form Yaupon is an upright oval to rounded large shrub to small tree 15 to 20 (sometimes up to 30) feet tall and wide; it may take single-stemmed or clump form.

Uses Specimen tree, patio tree, espalier, screen, tall hedge

Ornamental Attributes This underutilized broadleaf evergreen tree has small, rich green leaves and oodles of scarlet berries from late summer through winter.

Tolerances Drought, flood, salt, acidic soil, moderate air pollution

Growing Tips Yaupon prefers average to humus-rich neutral to acidic soil in full sun or partial shade, but it is widely tolerant of soil types and moisture levels. It is dioecious, and male and female clones are needed for fruit set. Female plants can also be pollinated by other species in the genus *Ilex*. This pest-free tree grows fairly quickly to 10 to 15 feet, then slows down with age.

Cultivars and Related Species *Ilex vomitoria* 'Dodd's Yellow' and 'Katherine' are heavily fruited with yellow berries; 'Pendula' is stunning, with an upright

trunk, gracefully weeping branches, and dense fruit set. *I. opaca,* American holly, has spiny olive-green leaves and rich red berries on slow-growing, spreading to conical plants 15 to 50 feet tall. It is native from Massachusetts and Missouri south to Florida and Texas (Zones 5 to 8). *I.* × 'Nellie R. Steven' (Zones 6 to 9) is a hybrid with glossy black-green leaves with scattered spines and large red berries on upright oval plants 15 to 40 feet tall.

Juniperus virginiana | Eastern Red Cedar, Old Field Juniper

Native Habitat and Range Woodland edges, old fields, meadows, and rocky ground from Nova Scotia, Ontario, south to Georgia, Iowa

Hardiness and Cultivated Range Zones 4 to 9; Nova Scotia, British Columbia, south to Georgia, New Mexico, northern California

Landscape Form This conical to upright, oval to rounded tree is small to midsize, growing 40 to 60 feet tall and 10 to 20 feet wide.

Uses Specimen tree, topiary, screen, tall hedge

Ornamental Attributes This dense, conical conifer has deep green fine- to medium-textured awllike needles and grayish to reddish-brown bark that exfoliates in long, ragged strips.

Tolerances Drought, heat, wind, salt, alkaline soil, acidic soil, moderate air pollution

Growing Tips Plant eastern red cedar in average to humus-rich, well-drained soil in full sun or partial shade. When young, it grows moderately fast to 15 to 20 feet; growth slows with age. It is dioecious, with female plants forming blue-gray berries. Plants may be susceptible to *Gymnosporangium* rust, which produces globular red growths on the branches.

Cultivars and Related Species *Juniperus virginiana* 'Emerald Sentinel' is a narrow, columnar selection with deep green needles; 'Grey Owl', 'Manhattan Blue', and 'Silver Spreader' have blue-gray needles. *J. flaccida,* drooping juniper, is a graceful oval tree to 50 feet with weeping branch tips. Native from south-central Texas into Mexico (Zones 7 to 10), it thrives only where summer humidity is low. *J. scopulorum,* Rocky Mountain juniper, is the western counterpart of eastern red cedar and performs better in the west. Native from Alberta to Texas, west to British Columbia, eastern Washington, and Arizona (Zones 3 to 7), it is noted for its narrow, upright form and gray-green to blue needles. 'Gray Gleam', 'Moonglow', 'Skyrocket', and 'Wichita Blue' are a few good blue selections.

Lagerstroemia indica | Common Crape Myrtle

Native Habitat and Range Woodland edges, clearings, and rock outcroppings in China, Korea

Hardiness and Cultivated Range Zones 7 to 10; Virginia, Missouri, British Columbia, south to Florida, New Mexico, California

Landscape Form This upright, oval to rounded, small to midsize tree, 15 to 30 (sometimes to 40) feet tall and wide, may take single-stemmed or clump form.

Uses Specimen tree, shade tree, screen, container plant

Ornamental Attributes Crape myrtle's trusses of colorful white, pink, or red summer flowers last for months, fol-

Tall, dense, and evergreen, eastern red cedar works well as a screening hedge. When deciding between an informal and a formal hedge, remember that formal hedges require a good eye and a commitment to regular pruning.

Planted in a row, common crape myrtles form an openwork screen, their colorful bark on sinuous stems beautifully highlighted under a diaphanous canopy. Used individually, a single specimen creates a billowing ceiling in a small garden room.

lowed by globular seedpods. Its small elliptic to oval leaves turn yellow, orange, or red in late autumn, and its sinuous trunks often have exfoliating tan and cinnamon bark.

Tolerances Moderate drought, moderate air pollution

Growing Tips Plant crape myrtle in average to humus-rich neutral to acidic soil in full sun or light shade. When young, it quickly reaches 15 to 20 feet; growth moderates with age, depending on the cultivar. Many dwarf to compact cultivars are available for small garden rooms. It can be killed to the ground in sudden cold snaps but will often resprout from the roots, ultimately regrowing into a multistemmed tree. It may be susceptible to powdery mildew and aphids.

Cultivars and Related Species Cultivars of *Lagerstroemia indica* number in the hundreds. A few popular ones include 'Dynamite', which is cherry-red and mildew resistant; 'Hopi' is a clear pink dwarf to eight feet; 'Muskogee' is lavender with red fall color; 'Natchez' is white with cinnamon bark and orange fall color. *L. fauriei,* cinnamon-barked crape myrtle, is a large, fast-growing tree to 30 feet tall and wide with a graceful, arching form and rich cinnamon-red bark and fragrant white flowers. It is native to China (Zones 6 to 9).

Native Alternative None

Magnolia stellata | Star Magnolia

Native Habitat and Range Forest edges, moist woodlands, and clearings in Japan

Hardiness and Cultivated Range Zones 4 to 9; Nova Scotia, British Columbia, south to Georgia, New Mexico, California

Landscape Form Star magnolia is an upright, oval to rounded, small to midsize tree, 15 to 20 feet tall and wide, with branches close to the ground and a twiggy crown.

Uses A lovely patio or shade tree if limbed up

Ornamental Attributes Fragrant, pure white, star-shaped flowers with up to 15 petals open in early spring. Star magnolia's elongated oval to somewhat spatula-shaped medium green leaves turn yellow to russet in autumn, and its woolly flower buds are decorative in winter.

Tolerances Moderate drought, heat, moderate air pollution, alkaline soil

Growing Tips Plant star magnolia in full sun or light shade in moist, well-drained humus-rich soil. When young, it grows fairly slowly to 10 to 15 feet; growth slows more with age. Place the

tree in a protected spot that stays cool, since warm microclimates encourage early flowering and may lead to bud loss caused by late frost. It has no serious pests.

Cultivars and Related Species *Magnolia stellata* 'Jane Platt' has light pink flowers; 'Royal Star' has pink buds that open to white blooms; 'Rubra' has dark pink flowers; 'Waterlily' is white with up to 32 petals. *M. kobus,* kobus magnolia (Zones 4 to 8), is a large version of star magnolia, 30 to 40 feet tall with a rounded crown, whose flowers have fewer, thick petals. *M. × loebneri,* loebner magnolia (Zones 4 to 9), is a fast-growing hybrid of the above two species with an upright crown to 30 feet and large, elliptical leaves; the flowers of 'Leonard Messel' have pink-stained petals that are white on the inside; 'Merrill' is a popular free-flowering white selection.

Native Alternatives *Magnolia ashei,* Ashe's magnolia, has huge, tropical-looking leathery leaves and large beaker-shaped white flowers on an irregular crown 15 to 30 feet tall. It is noted for blooming when quite young. Native from Florida to Texas (Zones 6 to 9), *M. macrophylla, M. fraseri,* and *M. tripetala* are similar species, also with deciduous foliage. *Magnolia* 'Elizabeth' is one of many yellow-flowered hybrids with the native *M. acuminata* as a parent. Hardy in Zones 5 to 9, it blooms in midspring on naked branches, followed by lush, midsize leaves.

Branches start low on 'Royal Star' star magnolia. If you desire, you can remove the lower limbs on young trees to create space for a planting of herbaceous perennials underneath.

The fragrant flowers of sweetbay open in late spring to early summer. This native tree can be grown as a single-stemmed midsize tree or as a multistemmed clump. It is also beautiful as an unusual container plant on the patio.

Magnolia virginiana | Sweetbay, Swamp Magnolia

Native Habitat and Range Low woods, swamps, and streambanks from Massachusetts to Florida, west to Texas

Hardiness and Cultivated Range Zones 6 to 9; coastal New England, Indiana, British Columbia, south to Florida, New Mexico, California

Landscape Form An upright, oval to rounded, small to midsize tree, 20 to 40 feet tall and 10 to 15 feet wide, sweetbay may take single-stemmed or clump form.

Uses Specimen tree, patio tree, screen, container plant

Ornamental Attributes Fragrant creamy-white chalices open in late spring and early summer. The lush, leathery, elongated oval leaves are sea-green in summer and russet to yellow in autumn.

Tolerances Flooding, soil compaction, salt, moderate air pollution

Growing Tips Plant sweetbay in humus-rich acidic soil in full sun or shade. It has a moderate growth rate when young to 15 to 20 feet; growth slows with age. It has no serious pests.

Cultivars and Related Species *Magnolia virginiana* var. *australis* is usually single-stemmed, upright, and regular with evergreen to semievergreen foliage in the North. Though *M. grandiflora*, bullbay magnolia, is a giant evergreen tree too large for most gardens, the selection 'Little Gem' is compact, with small, neat leaves. It is slow growing and fits well into intimate spaces.

Malus floribunda | Japanese Crabapple

Native Habitat and Range Woodland edges, clearings in Japan

Hardiness and Cultivated Range Zones 3 to 7; Nova Scotia, British Columbia, south to Georgia, New Mexico, northern California

Landscape Form A broadly oval to rounded, small to midsize tree, 15 to 25 feet tall and 20 to 30 feet wide, Japanese crabapple is single-stemmed with low branches.

Uses Specimen tree, patio tree if pruned up

Ornamental Attributes Pink buds open to fragrant white flowers, followed by pendant red fruits. The elliptic leaves turn yellow to russet in autumn.

Tolerances Drought, heat, moderate soil compaction, salt

Growing Tips Plant Japanese crabapple in average to humus-rich neutral to mildly acidic soil in full sun or light shade. It has a moderate growth rate to 15 to 20 feet and slows with age. It may be susceptible to fire blight, canker, and scab. *Gymnosporangium* rust is problematic in some plants; selections are resistant.

Cultivars and Related Species *Malus sargentii,* Sargent's crabapple (Zones 4 to 7), is a tight-crowned species to 15 feet tall and wide with stiff branches lined with clustered white flowers. Hundreds of species and hybrids are available. Flower color varies from white to pink

to rose-red, and fruits may be red, orange, or yellow. 'Donald Wyman' is an old but excellent selection with good disease resistence, white flowers, and red fruits.

Native Alternative *Malus ioensis,* prairie crabapple, is a lovely open-crowned tree to 30 feet tall and wide with large white flowers and green fruits. It is native from Indiana and Minnesota south to Arkansas and Oklahoma (Zones 4 to 8).

Parkinsonia florida (syn. *Cercidium floridum*) | Blue Paloverde

Native Habitat and Range Stream edges, arroyos, and riverbanks of the Sonoran desert of southeastern California, Arizona, Mexico

Hardiness and Cultivated Range Zones 8 to 10; Florida, Southwest from Texas to California, Nevada

Landscape Form Blue paloverde is a broadly oval to rounded, small to midsize tree, 20 to 25 feet tall and 25 to 30

Left: The Japanese crabapple cultivar 'Snowdrift' produces pink buds that open to fragrant white flowers. These are followed by dangling orange-red fruits that persist through winter.

Right: In gardens of the arid West, the lithe green branches of blue paloverde create an appealing light screen that opens up even more in the summer as the tree drops its small leaves during the hottest months.

Plant lacebark pine in a spot where you can admire its striking exfoliating bark up close. To offer a better view of the bark, you may remove some of the lower branches, but don't try to fill the open space with herbaceous plants—few will grow under a pine tree.

feet wide; it may be single-stemmed with low branches or grow as a clump.

Uses Specimen tree, patio tree if pruned up

Ornamental Attributes Showy yellow flowers smother the lithe branches in early spring and thin, beanlike pods form in summer. The small, scalelike leaves drop as summer heats up, but the tree's branches are green, as are the trunks of young to middle-aged trees, and photosynthesize when the leaves are absent.

Tolerances Drought, extreme heat, high wind, moderate salt

Growing Tips Plant blue paloverde in average to sandy, well-drained neutral to alkaline soil in full sun. Though hardy and relatively pest-free, it is intolerant of heavy or wet soil and performs best in the low humidity of the West. It

quickly reaches 10 to 15 feet, then slows in growth with age. Plants branch to the ground, so they must be pruned into tree form for most garden situations.

Cultivars and Related Species
Parkinsonia microphylla, little-leaf or yellow paloverde (Zones 8 to 10), is a large shrub to small tree with dense branches to 12 feet tall and wide that blooms in late spring and early summer. Native to the desert Southwest, it is very drought tolerant.

Pinus bungeana | Lacebark Pine

Native Habitat and Range Woodlands and clearings in China

Hardiness and Cultivated Range Zones 5 to 7; New England, Illinois, British Columbia, south to Georgia, New Mexico, California

Observe your young Chinese pistache closely as it grows, and stake, train, and prune it as needed to attain a pleasing, even form.

Landscape Form This pyramidal to broad, teardrop-shaped evergreen tree is 30 to 50 feet tall and 25 to 35 feet wide.

Uses Specimen tree

Ornamental Attributes Lacebark pine has a beautiful upright form with airy, deep green needles and exfoliating green, brown, and tan bark.

Tolerances Drought, alkaline soil

Growing Tips Plant lacebark pine in average to humus-rich, well-drained neutral soil in full sun. It should be transplanted in spring or late summer, not in autumn. It is a slow-growing tree, with susceptibility to root rot and pollution.

Cultivars and Related Species *Pinus densiflora,* Japanese red pine, is an irregular form to 40 to 60 feet with numerous named selections of smaller stature. It is native to China, Japan, and Korea (Zones 3 to 7). Native to southern Europe (Zones 3 to 8), *P. mugo,* mugo pine, is a small, dense species 10 to 15 feet tall and wide with lush needles.

Native Alternative *Pinus aristata,* bristle-cone pine, is a drought-tolerant, compact species native to the Sierras (Zones 4 to 7) and noted for being the longest living organism. It has dense, short needles and is very slow growing to 20 feet. Choose it for a container or as a focal point next to a bench.

Pistacia chinensis | Chinese Pistache

Native Habitat and Range Woodland edges and clearings in China, Taiwan, the Philippines

Hardiness and Cultivated Range Zones 6 to 9; coastal New England to Missouri, British Columbia, south to Florida, Texas, California

Landscape Form This upright, oval to rounded, small to midsize tree grows 30 to 40 feet tall and 25 to 35 feet wide; it is single-stemmed with upswept branches.

Uses Specimen tree, shade tree

Ornamental Attributes The flowers of Chinese pistache are insignificant but followed by globose fruits in multicolored clusters ranging from sky-blue to red. The tree has furrowed to scaly bark, and its pinnately divided leaves are lustrous in summer, flaming red-orange in autumn.

Tolerances Drought, heat, soil compaction, moderate air pollution

Growing Tips Plant this pest-free tree in moist, humus-rich neutral to acidic soil in full sun or light shade. Medium to fast growing when young, it quickly reaches 15 to 25 feet. Young trees need pruning and shaping as they grow to encourage a pleasing, even form.

Cultivars and Related Species *Pistacia chinensis* 'Keith Davey' has a more regular habit than the species.

Native Alternatives Native from Texas to Arizona (Zones 7 to10), *Fraxinus greggii*, little-leaf ash, is a large shrub to small tree to 20 feet, suitable for patios and large containers. *F. cuspidata*, fragrant ash, is a graceful 20-foot tree with bright green foliage and fragrant, showy flower clusters in spring. It is native to the Southwest (Zones 8 to10).

Populus tremuloides
Quaking Aspen

Native Habitat and Range Woodland edges, old fields, and clearings from Newfoundland across the subarctic to Alaska, British Columbia, south to Pennsylvania, Iowa, mountains of New Mexico, California

Hardiness and Cultivated Range Zones 1 to 6 (cooler parts of Zone 7); subarctic Canada, south to Virginia, New Mexico, northern California

Landscape Form A narrow, upright oval, small to midsize tree 30 to 60 feet tall and 20 to 30 feet wide, quaking aspen is usually single-stemmed but may take a clump form.

Uses Specimen tree, shade tree, patio tree, screen

Ornamental Attributes The leaves, which are oval to rhomboidal and turn clear yellow in fall, have long, flattened petioles that enable them to move freely, quaking in the wind. The tan to creamy-white bark is smooth with dark nodes.

Tolerances Moderate drought, extreme wind and cold, moderate salt, moderate air pollution

Growing Tips Plant quaking aspen in average to humus-rich, well-drained neutral to acidic soil in full sun or partial shade. Very fast growing when young and quickly reaching 20 to 40 feet, it is fast to moderate growing with age. The tree has weak wood and is short-lived, generally 40 to 60 years. Canker and mildew are problems, mostly when it is grown outside its native range.

Cultivars and Related Species *Populus grandidentata,* big-tooth aspen, is a more southerly species and as a result more heat tolerant. It grows taller and stouter than *P. tremuloides*—60 to 90 feet tall—with beige- to green-tinted bark, and its leaves are larger, with scalloped to shallowly toothed margins. It is native from Newfoundland and Manitoba south to Virginia, Kentucky, and Iowa (Zones 3 to 7).

Prosopis glandulosa var. *glandulosa* | Honey Mesquite

Native Habitat and Range Intermittent streams, arroyos, and riverbanks from Kansas, Texas, west to New Mexico, Mexico

Hardiness and Cultivated Range Zones 7 to 10; desert Southwest, southern Great Plains, California

Landscape Form This broad, oval to rounded to weeping tree may be small to midsize, growing to 20 to 25 feet tall and 25 to 30 feet wide. It can be single-stemmed with low branches or grow as a clump with an irregularly branching form.

Right: Narrow and upright, quaking aspen looks especially attractive when several specimens are planted in a group.

Uses Specimen tree, patio tree, screen

Ornamental Attributes The showy, fragrant dense spikes of cream flowers are borne at the nodes in spring and produce tough, beanlike pods in summer. The tree's branches are spiny, and its lush, bright green pinnately divided leaves drop as summer heats up.

Tolerances Extreme drought, extreme heat, high wind, moderate salt

Growing Tips Intolerant of heavy or wet soil, honey mesquite should be planted in average sandy to humusy, well-drained neutral to alkaline soil in full sun. Since this tree has a taproot, transplant it only when young. It has a moderate growth rate when young to 10 to 15 feet; growth slows with age. It branches to the ground, so it must be pruned into tree form for most garden situations. It is relatively pest-free.

Cultivars and Related Species Native from California and Utah south to Texas and Mexico (Zones 7 to 10), *Prosopis pubescens,* screwbean mesquite, is a small, mounded deciduous tree to 15 feet with spiraling pods that bestow its common name. *P. velutina,* velvet mesquite, is a handsome, mounding tree 10 to 20 feet tall and 30 feet wide with a gnarled, picturesque trunk and branches and ferny, deciduous foliage. It is native from Texas and California to Mexico (Zones 8 to 10).

Prunus × *yedoensis* Yoshino Cherry

Native Habitat and Range Hybrid species of garden origin; wild forms usually found along woodland edges and in clearings

Hardiness and Cultivated Range Zones 5 to 8; Nova Scotia, Illinois, British Columbia, south to Georgia, New Mexico, California

Landscape Form An upright, oval to rounded small to midsize tree, 20 to 40 feet tall and 20 to 30 feet wide, Yoshino cherry may take a single-stemmed or clump form.

Uses Specimen tree, shade tree, patio tree

Ornamental Attributes In spring, showy pink buds open to white flowers on bare branches, and the tree's rich green leaves turn apricot, orange, or burgundy in autumn. It has glossy gray bark.

Tolerances Moderate drought

Growing Tips Plant Yoshino cherry in average to humus-rich, well-drained neutral to moderately acidic soil in full sun or light shade. Fast growing when

A tough tree for arid climates, honey mesquite has a taproot and should only be moved while it is young. It branches to the ground, so it needs to be pruned if it is to look more treelike.

For a few fleeting days each spring, the rounded canopy of small-growing Yoshino cherry is covered with delicate flowers. Compared with other Japanese flowering cherries, it is relatively pest- and disease-free.

young, it quickly reaches 20 to 30 feet; growth is moderate with age. Though cherries are often susceptible to fire blight, borers, and canker, among other pests, and as a result usually live only 15 to 30 years, Yoshino is relatively pest- and disease-free.

Cultivars and Related Species *Prunus* 'Hally Jolivette', a fantastic hybrid with higan cherry, is a small tree with a broad, oval crown. It is heat tolerant, disease resistant and hardy in Zones 5 to 7. *P. × subhirtella,* higan cherry, is grown in two forms: *P. × subhirtella* 'Jugatsu-zakura', which flowers in autumn and spring and has a wide, rounded crown; and *P. pendula,* which has an upright trunk and gracefully weeping branches. Both are native to Japan (Zones 5 to 8). *P. mume,*

flowering apricot, native to China and Japan (Zones 6 to 9), blooms during winter warm spells and has intensely fragrant pink or white flowers.

Native Alternative *Prunus virginiana,* chokecherry, is a midsize tree to 25 feet with fragrant panicles of white flowers in spring. The elliptical foliage turns orange to burgundy in autumn. It is native throughout the East and Midwest (Zones 3 to 7).

Quercus virginiana
Virginia Live Oak

Native Habitat and Range Woodland edges, clearings, and shores from coastal regions of Virginia, south to Florida, west to Texas, Mexico

Zones 8 to 9; roughly that of its native distribution

Landscape Form This broadly oval to rounded picturesque tree is midsize to large, 40 to 80 feet tall and 60 to 100 feet wide; it is usually single-stemmed and low-branching but may also be multistemmed.

Uses Specimen tree, shade tree, wind-break, screen

Ornamental Attributes Virginia live oak has dark evergreen foliage with silvery undersides that densely clothe the rounded, umbrellalike crown.

Tolerances Drought, heat, soil com-paction, salt, moderate air pollution

How to Grow Virginia live oak prefers average to humus-rich, well-drained acidic soil in full sun but tolerates sand or clay. The tree is best moved when young. It has a moderate growth rate when young to 20 to 30 feet; growth slows with age. Oak wilt is rare in this species, but it has been reported.

Cultivars and Related Species *Quercus virginiana* 'Gardenview Gold' has golden-yellow foliage; 'Highrise' is upright with a dense crown. *Q. chrysolepis,* canyon live oak, is a drought- and heat-tolerant large evergreen species with hollylike leaves; it is native from the arid Southwest through California to Oregon (Zones 7 to 9). *Q. turbinella,* scrub oak, is a drought- and heat-tolerant small evergreen species with blue-green leaves native from Texas through California and Utah (Zones 6 to 9).

Left: North American native Virginia live oak requires a lot of space to accommodate its large, spreading canopy. As it can easily overwhelm a smaller piece of land, the tree should only be planted where it has room to spread its gnarly, picturesque branches.

Stewartia pseudocamellia
Japanese Stewartia

Native Habitat and Range Woodlands, forest edges, and clearings in Japan

Hardiness and Cultivated Range Zones 5 to 7; New England, Illinois, British Columbia, south to North Carolina, New Mexico, northern California

Landscape Form This upright, oval to pyramidal midsize tree is 20 to 40 feet (sometimes up to 60 feet) tall and 10 to 20 feet wide; it is usually single-stemmed but may branch close to the ground.

Uses Specimen tree, patio tree

Ornamental Attributes Japanese stewartia bears delicate white, cup-shaped early-summer flowers with yellow stamens; flowers resemble a single rose or camel-lia. In fall the midgreen pointed oval foliage ignites in fiery hues of orange, red, and yellow, setting off the patchy, exfoliating cream, rust, and orange bark.

Tolerances Slight drought

Growing Tips Plant this tree in full sun or partial shade in evenly moist, well-drained humus-rich soil that is neutral to acidic. When it is young, water it well in summer to keep its leaves from scorching; as it matures the amount of summer watering can be reduced. It tends to grow slowly, to 20 to 30 feet, when young, and it slows down even more with age. Its hardiness is variable and not fully established, so experiment.

Cultivars and Related Species *Stewartia koreana,* Korean stewartia, has larger flowers than its Japanese cousin. *S. monodelpha,* tall stewartia, is an upright tree to 60 feet that branches horizontally as it ages. It has decorative cinnamon-colored bark and is native to Japan (Zones 5 to 8).

A wonderful presence in the garden, medium-sized Japanese stewartia shows off large camellia-like flowers in early summer, bright fall color, and striking exfoliating bark that's attractive all year long.

Native Alternative A native of Virginia and Arkansas, south to Florida and Texas (Zones 7 to 9), *Stewartia malacodendron,* silky stewartia, is an excellent species for the Southeast. If kept clear of soggy soils, it grows slowly into an open-crowned small tree 10 to 15 feet tall and wide with huge snowy flowers to 4 inches across.

Styrax japonicus | Japanese Snowbell

Native Habitat and Range Woodland understories in Japan, Korea, China

Hardiness and Cultivated Range Zones 5 to 8; New England, Illinois, British Columbia, south to North Carolina, New Mexico, northern California

Landscape Form This broadly oval to rounded, small to midsize tree grows 20 to 30 feet tall and wide and usually takes a single-stemmed and low-branching form.

Uses Specimen tree, patio tree

Ornamental Attributes This elegant small tree has pendant clusters of five-petaled white bells in late spring. Its bright green elliptic leaves turn pale yellow in autumn; winter reveals smooth gray bark that fissures with age.

Tolerances Moderate drought

Growing Tips Plant Japanese snowbell in moist, well-drained, fertile, neutral to acidic soil in full sun or partial shade. Transplant it only in spring. It grows moderately fast to ten feet when young, then slows with age. Once established, this pest-free tree requires little care.

Right: An elegant small tree, Japanese snowbell draws attention with its pendulous flowers in late spring.

Framing a garden bench, tree lilacs create a pleasant, and, when in flower, fragrant retreat in a quiet corner of the garden.

Cultivars and Related Species *Styrax japonicus* 'Emerald Pagoda' is a more heat- and humidity-tolerant cultivar with an ascending, vase-shaped form, large lustrous leaves, and one-inch flowers. 'Pink Chimes' is similar in size and shape and bears a profusion of pale rose-pink flowers. *S. obassia* is a larger cousin that reaches 40 feet with an upright to columnar shape. The bold leaves are oval to rounded with a few terminal teeth, and the large fragrant flowers are carried in long chains.

Native Alternative *Styrax americanus,* American snowbell, slowly reaches 8 to 12 feet tall and 10 to 15 feet wide. Nodding, four-petaled white flowers hang in clusters below the medium green leaves in late spring. It is native from Virginia and Missouri, south to Florida and Louisiana (Zones 5 to 9).

Syringa reticulata | Tree Lilac

Native Habitat and Range Woodland edges, rock outcroppings, and clearings in Japan

Hardiness and Cultivated Range Zones 3 to 7; Nova Scotia, British Columbia, south to Georgia, New Mexico, northern California

Landscape Form This upright, oval to rounded small tree grows 20 to 30 feet tall and 15 to 20 feet wide; it may be single-stemmed, low branching, or clump forming.

Uses Specimen tree, patio tree, screen

Ornamental Attributes Large trusses of creamy-white flowers, slightly ill-scented, appear in early summer after other lilacs have bloomed. In autumn, the large, nearly heart-shaped leaves turn yellow; in winter the tree displays an eccentric to gnarly silhouette.

Tolerances Drought, cold, wind, alkaline soil, slight air pollution

Growing Tips Plant tree lilac in average to humus-rich neutral to alkaline soil in full sun or partial shade. It grows at a medium rate to 10 feet and slows with age. It is relatively trouble-free for a lilac but may be susceptible to powdery mildew, leaf spot, and borer.

Cultivars and Related Species *Syringa reticulata* 'Regent' is an upright, vigorous selection; 'Summer Snow' is a floriferous selection with a compact, rounded crown. *S. villosa,* late lilac, is a large shrub to 10 feet tall and wide that can be pruned into tree form. Lilac-colored to white flowers open in early summer and have a slight fragrance of lilac. It is native to China (Zones 3 to 7). *S. vulgaris,* common lilac, is a large shrub, often trained as a tree, with intoxicatingly fragrant purple, lilac, or white flowers in dense, showy trusses. This native of southern Europe (Zones 3 to 7) has many cultivars that highlight attributes varying from flower color to disease resistance.

Native Alternatives Found throughout the eastern and central U.S. (Zones 5 to 9), *Rhus copallina*, winged sumac, has large clusters of creamy flowers in summer that look similar to those of tree lilac. The foliage is pinnately divided, unlike the simple leaves of tree lilac. It grows as a spreading shrub but will reach 10 to 12 feet and can be pruned into tree form. *Holodiscus discolor,* ocean spray, is a large, open-crowned shrub with pendant clusters of foamy, cream-colored flowers. It is native from the Rocky Mountains west (Zones 4 to 8).

Shrubs

Abutilon megapotamicum
Flowering Maple, Chinese Lantern

Native Habitat and Range Tropical forest and mountainsides in southern Brazil

Hardiness and Cultivated Range Zones 8 to 10; coastal Southeast, Gulf Coast west to California, Pacific Northwest, southern British Columbia

Landscape Form This evergreen or semi-evergreen, arching shrub reaches six to ten feet in height and width in the wild but is much smaller in cultivation. Some forms are erect; others are fairly prostrate, acting more like horizontally challenged vines. The bright green leaves are lobed and maple-leaf-like.

Uses Screen, hedge, container plant

Ornamental Attributes Flowering maple is grown for its fabulous pendant, bell-shaped flowers with yellow petals and purple stamens protruding from crimson-red calyces, which bloom from summer through fall. Its foliage is also decorative, especially variegated selections.

Tolerances Heat

Growing Tips Plant flowering maple in full sun or light shade in fertile, moist, well-drained soil in a sheltered spot. It becomes sulky and resentful if allowed to dry out. Deadheading will prolong the bloom season and the plant's overall longevity. An older plant can be rejuvenated by cutting it back to the ground in late winter. If cold weather causes dieback, it may come back from the root.

Cultivars and Related Species *Abutilon megapotamicum* 'Variegatum', of garden origin, has green leaves mottled and speckled with yellow. Large, sunny-yellow bells dangle from the stems of *A.* 'Canary Bird', native to southern Brazil. *A. pictum,* the most significant parent of the *Abutilon* hybrids, is upright with deeply lobed leaves and orange bells and can become a 12- to 15-foot-tall shrub or small tree; *A. pictum* 'Thompsonii' has leaves splashed with yellow and peachy-coral-veined flowers. The blooms of *A.* × *hybridum* 'Nabob' are an indescribable shade of black raspberry–red.

Native Alternative *Acer circinatum,* vine maple, is a small deciduous tree or large shrub with palmately lobed leaves and brilliant red to orange autumn color. Plants grow 8 to 20 feet tall in open woods and forest edges from Alaska south to California (Zones 5 to 9).

Left: Grown for its attractive bell-shaped flowers, flowering maple comes in several forms. Some are erect, growing to six feet, others are more prostrate.

Arctostaphylos densiflora
'Howard McMinn' | 'Howard McMinn' Manzanita

Native Habitat and Range Selection from endangered, protected wild stands of *Arctostaphylos densiflora,* native to relic sand dunes in the Sonoma Valley, California

Hardiness and Cultivated Range Zones 8 to 10; west of Sierras and Cascades from southwestern British Columbia to southern California

Landscape Form This evergreen forms a mounding shrub five to seven feet high and six to ten feet wide with a dense, twiggy structure and twisted trunks.

Uses Specimen plant, hedge

Ornamental Attributes Showy pink flower clusters resembling those of heather clothe the plants in spring and are favored by hummingbirds and butterflies. The small red fruits appear in fall and were used by indigenous people in California in making pemmican. The shrub's distinctive reddish-brown bark on gnarly twisted trunks is attractive year-round.

Tolerances Drought, salt, sandy to clay soils

Growing Tips Although best grown in full sun in well-drained acidic soil, this most adaptable of the manzanitas can tolerate partial shade. Though durable, these plants cannot tolerate wet feet. Prune them judiciously to control overall size.

Cultivars and Related Species The most easily recognized member of the genus is *Arctostaphylos uva-ursi,* bearberry or kinnikinick, which is used as an evergreen groundcover. Native to subarctic North America south to New Jersey, Minnesota, and California (Zones 2 to 6), it grows one to two feet high and up to five feet wide in both full sun and partial shade. Another ground hugger is *A. nummularia* 'Small Change', whose shiny, dark green, finely fretted foliage adds luster to garden rooms in partial shade in Zones 7 to 10.

Aronia arbutifolia | Red Chokeberry

Native Habitat and Range Swamps, woodland clearings, wetland forests, and outcroppings from New England to Florida, west to Missouri, Texas

Hardiness and Cultivated Range Zones 4 to 9; eastern and southern U.S.; Pacific Northwest

Landscape Form This upright, deciduous shrub reaching ten feet tall and six feet wide has a tendency to sucker and form dense clumps.

Uses Informal hedge or hedgerow

The flowers of 'Howard McMinn' manzanita are popular with hummingbirds and butterflies: Place a seat nearby and watch.

With a tendency to sucker and form a dense clump, red chokeberry needs room to spread. Bearing more and larger fruit than the species, the cultivar 'Brilliantissima', shown here, serves as a first-class bird magnet in fall and winter, so be sure to plant it where you can watch the activity.

Ornamental Attributes White flowers appear in midspring as the deep green foliage unfurls. Chokeberry has great presence in fall and winter and acts as a bird attractant: The glossy red fruits persist into the winter long after the crimson-red leaves have fallen.

Tolerances Drought, wet or compacted soil, salt

Growing Tips Chokeberry thrives in full sun or partial shade in acidic soil. (Optimum fruiting and fall color occurs in full sun.) It tolerates wet or dry soil conditions but won't perform in soils that are alkaline. To regenerate growth on established plants, cut back a third of the old shoots to the ground after flowering.

Cultivars and Related Species *Aronia arbutifolia* 'Brilliantissima' (Zones 3 to 9) bears more and larger fruits than the species and exhibits more vivid fall color. Persistent, shiny black berries and deep wine-red fall color are hallmarks of *A. melanocarpa,* an East Coast native (Zones 4 to 9) that reaches seven feet high by three feet wide; 'Autumn Magic' has larger, shinier black berries that hold well into the winter and grows six feet tall and ten feet wide.

Buxus sempervirens | Common or English Boxwood

Native Habitat and Range Woodland edges and clearings of southern Europe, Turkey, and North Africa

Hardiness and Cultivated Range Zones 5 to 8; New England, Southeast, Pacific Northwest, northern California, western and southern British Columbia

Landscape Form The classic hedging plant appears in many guises in

The foliage of evergreen common boxwood responds well to pruning and shaping and can be clipped into any shape imaginable, including a handsome formal hedge that provides privacy and an elegant backdrop for many types of plantings. Bear in mind, though, that maintaining a formal hedge requires plenty of dedication and patience.

American gardens. Shiny, lustrous dark green leaves adorn plants that may be clipped into just about any shape imaginable, from balls and pyramids to fantastic topiary forms. If left untended, boxwood forms a dense, rounded mound that may reach a height and width of 15 feet.

Uses Hedges of all sizes from tall background screens to short outlines for parterres and knot gardens

Ornamental Attributes The deep green summer foliage of this broad-leafed evergreen becomes bronze in the winter and responds well to pruning and shaping.

Tolerances Moderate drought, severe regenerative pruning, animal browse (deer resistant; leaves and stems toxic to livestock)

Growing Tips Boxwood prefers fertile, well-drained soil and partial shade and can be sited in full sun if the soil isn't allowed to dry out. Prune hedges, topiaries, and other shaped boxwood in mid- to late summer. Cutting back hard to rejuvenate an older or unkempt hedge should be done in spring.

Cultivars and Related Species *Buxus sempervirens* 'Graham Blandy' has an upright, columnar habit that works in containers, as a hedging plant, or placed as a focal point or vertical accent up to six feet tall and two to three feet in diameter. *B. sempervirens* 'Marginata' has dark green leaves edged with a band of yellow; left unpruned it will grow to eight feet high and ten feet wide. Slow growing and more compact than the species, *B. sempervirens* 'Suffruticosa' can be used for small hedges and edging. *B. microphylla* 'Green Pillow' (Zones 6 to 10) is very compact and dense, forming a small, roundish ball 1½ high by 3 feet wide.

Native Alternative *Myrica gale,* sweet gale, is a dense, rounded to broadly oval semi-evergreen shrub with fragrant, narrowly oval leaves and dusky berries. It thrives on the edges of wetlands and in moist, sunny areas in Zones 3 to 8.

Callicarpa americana | American Beautyberry, American Beauty Bush

Native Habitat and Range Meadows, dunes, and open, well-drained wood-lands from Maryland to Missouri, south to Florida, Texas

Hardiness and Cultivated Range Zones 6 to 10; southern coastal New England, Missouri, and British Columbia, south to Florida, Texas, California

Landscape Form Beautyberry grows six to eight feet tall and has a slightly vase-shaped open habit with branches facing outward. Its somewhat coarse, toothed leaves may reach eight inches in length.

Uses Mass planting for optimal fall effect

Ornamental Attributes The tiny, insignificant lavender cymes borne in clusters around the stem produce luscious drupes in showstopping magenta in autumn. The distinctive fruits lure birds to feed in late fall and early winter.

Tolerances Drought, salt, poor soils

Growing Tips For optimum results, plant beautyberry in full sun to partial shade (full sun for more fruit) in well-drained fertile soil; however, it can also tolerate dry, rocky sites and sandy soil. Once established, the shrub requires little water or pruning and is very pest and

Plant American beautyberry in a spot that needs a touch of brilliant color in fall. The distinctive berries will last until early winter before being gobbled up by hungry birds.

disease resistant. It bears more fruit if planted in groups.

Cultivars and Related Species *Callicarpa americana* var. *lactea* bears luminous white drupes. *C. bodinieri* var. *giraldii* 'Profusion' is bushy and erect, topping out at over ten feet, with metallic violet fruit. Native to China and Japan, purple beautyberry, *C. dichotoma,* has an arching, elegant habit and grows four feet tall and four to six feet wide, with sparkling violet-purple drupes encircling the stems above the foliage; 'Albifructus' reaches eight feet and bears white fruits.

A broadleaf evergreen with lustrous dark green leaves, autumn camellia flowers in late fall to early winter, as its name suggests. Cultivars can be tall and elegant or compact and shrubby, making this a versatile choice for a small garden.

Camellia sasanqua | Autumn Camellia, Sasanqua Camellia

Native Habitat and Range Woodland understory from northern Japan to the Ryukyu Islands

Hardiness and Cultivated Range Zones 7 to 9; mid-Atlantic and the Southeast; Pacific Northwest, northern California

Landscape Form Shiny, dark evergreen, reflective leaves clothe this plant, whose height at maturity ranges from 4 to 15 feet. Some cultivars are compact and shrubby; others are tall and elegant. There are also weeping forms, which can be employed as groundcovers.

Uses Hedges, espaliers on protected north- and east-facing walls

Ornamental Attributes This aristocratic camellia blooms in late autumn and early winter, displaying elegant single blooms in snowy white or palest blush pink.

Cultivars offer shades of richly hued rose and bright pink and flower forms that may be single, semidouble, or ruffled.

Tolerances Drought, heat

Growing Tips Like rhododendrons and azaleas, the sasanqua camellia prefers rich, organic, acidic soils, although it is able to tolerate a wide range of soil conditions. It also likes partial shade but can take full sun if supplemental water is provided. Mulch annually with organic matter such as composted leaf mold. If pruning is necessary, do it in early spring before buds are set.

Cultivars and Related Species *Camellia sasanqua* 'Setsugekka' is a classic single white with gold-yellow stamens; the frilly, bright candy-pink flowers of 'Shishigashira' are semidouble. *Camellia × vernalis* 'Yuletide', which salutes the holiday season with Christmas-red single

A drought-tolerant evergreen suitable to frost-free climates, California lilac can serve the function of a large shrub or a small tree. It works well on its own but also integrates nicely with other plants in an informal hedge or the wall in a garden room.

flowers, is more cold tolerant than *C. sasanqua* (Zones 7 to 9). There are over 2,000 cultivars of *Camellia japonica,* native to Japan, China, and Taiwan, which can form a shrub or small tree. Choose from a multitude of flower forms, colors, and sizes.

Native Alternative *Carpenteria californica* is an upright oval shrub found in the wild only in California (Zones 8 to 10). It has camellia-like flowers in early summer atop fuzzy evergreen foliage.

Ceanothus thysiflorus
California Lilac, Blue Brush, Blue Mountain Lilac

Native Habitat and Range Scrub, chapparal, wooded slopes, and canyons of California

Hardiness and Cultivated Range Zones 7 to 9; southwestern British Columbia

south to California west of the Cascades

Landscape Form This fast-growing large shrub or small tree has upright, arching branches and a shrubby habit. It grows 6 to 20 feet tall and 8 to 20 feet wide.

Uses Specimen plant, hedge, espalier

Ornamental Attributes The glossy, oval, dark green evergreen foliage is a foil for the bright blue, fragrant flowers borne in terminal and lateral panicles in late spring and early summer. In mild years some rebloom may occur in the autumn.

Tolerances Drought and heat, salt, sandy soil

Growing Tips Site California lilac in full sun in fertile, well-drained soil—wet feet or standing water means certain death from root rot. It can tolerate neutral or slightly alkaline soil and thrives in coastal situations away from the

Bearing attractive fragrant flowers for weeks in late summer when few other shrubs look their best, sweet pepperbush grows up to six feet high, effectively screening unattractive views or anything else that you may want to hide.

beach. Shape it by shearing after the bloom period ends.

Cultivars and Related Species *Ceanothus thysiflorus* 'Skylark' has inky, dark green leaves, bright blue flowers, and is hardy to 5°F. It is smaller than the species, reaching six feet in height and width. *C. thyrsiflorus* var. *repens* has a prostrate habit and is useful as a groundcover on hillsides and slopes. The deciduous shrub *C. × pallidus* 'Marie Simon' grows to five feet and has rich burgundy stems and an upright shape, with pale pink flowers in terminal panicles that bloom throughout the summer and autumn; *C. × delilianus* 'Henri Desfosse' is also deciduous and bears deep blue flowers over the course of the summer. *C. velutinus,* red root, is a wide, evergreen shrub with fragrant foliage native to the high plains, Rocky Mountains, and Sierra Nevada (Zones 5 to 8).

Clethra alnifolia | Sweet Pepperbush, Summersweet

Native Habitat and Range Along streams and in bogs and swamps in wet, sandy soil from Maine to northern Florida, eastern Texas

Hardiness and Cultivated Range Zones 4 to 9; New England, British Columbia, south to northern Florida, northern California

Landscape Form This deciduous clumping shrub has a slightly arching, rounded habit and grows six feet high and wide. The shallow root system suckers, forming dense clumps in moist soil.

Uses Mixed or tapestry hedge; privacy hedge for pond; garden room near the ocean

Ornamental Attributes From mid- to late summer, sweet pepperbush bears racemes of showy, creamy-white flowers that exude a sweetly spicy bouquet. The foliage turns golden-yellow in autumn.

Tolerances Moderate drought, waterlogging, damp soils, salt, fire

Growing Tips Sweet pepperbush, like its close heath and heather relatives, is intolerant of lime and should be planted in moist, acid-based soils. It performs best in light or dappled shade under a high canopy, although it can survive in full sun if given adequate water.

Cultivars and Related Species *Clethra alnifolia* 'Hummingbird' is a compact cultivar, two to three feet in height and width, good at the front of a border or as a groundcover. It presents fragrant white flowers in midsummer and has shiny, dark green leaves. 'Rosea' displays baby-pink flowers and does best in full sun; 'Ruby Spice' has the darkest pink flowers of all the cultivars. *C. barbinervis* hails from the mountains of Japan (Zones 5 to 8) and forms a large ten-foot shrub with exfoliating copper-rust-colored bark. The dark green leaves burst into flaming red and yellow with the onset of fall.

Cornus stolonifera | Red Osier Dogwood, Red Twig Dogwood

Native Habitat and Range Woodland riparian areas, swamps, low-lying meadows, floodplains, and wetlands in eastern North America

Hardiness and Cultivated Range Zones 2 to 9; Alaska, subarctic Canada, south to California, Florida, Texas

Landscape Form This upright, rounded, deciduous shrub grows six to eight feet tall and wide and has opposite, oval, bright green leaves. It tends to sucker, producing many-stemmed wide clumps.

Flowers and fruit of red osier dogwood are appealing, but the real reason for growing this shrub is its unobscured display of carmine-red stems all winter long.

Uses Informal hedge near a pond or stream, woodland edge

Ornamental Attributes In spring, small white flowers are displayed in flat-topped clusters that later produce white berries. The leaves turn orange-red in autumn, and in the winter, carmine-red stems and twigs add much-needed color in the garden.

Tolerances Wet soils, flooding, standing water, some tolerance to fire

Growing Tips Red osier dogwood thrives in rich, moist soils in partial to full sun. Rejuvenate the plant and encourage maximum winter color by coppicing or cutting all stems back to 12 to 18 inches in early spring every other year.

Cultivars and Related Species *Cornus stolonifera* 'Flaviramea' has green foliage and yellow winter color; 'Silver and Gold' sports apple-green foliage with

Often growing wider than tall, winter hazel is a fountainlike deciduous shrub that forms a wonderful understory layer in a garden room. Its delightful early-spring flowers are an added bonus.

white margins and bright yellow stems in winter. *C.* 'Kelseyii' is a dwarf cultivar only a foot tall and wide that stands out in the garden when the stems assume their wintry hue of fiery red. In late fall, cooler temperatures ignite the stems of *C.* 'Midwinter Fire' in hues of coppery-tan to orange; it can be coppiced, cut back, or pruned into a small tree 12 to 15 feet tall. It is hardy in Zones 6 to 8.

Corylopsis pauciflora | Winter Hazel

Native Habitat and Range Woodland understory in Japan and Taiwan

Hardiness and Cultivated Range Zones 6 to 9; Pacific Northwest, western British Columbia, southeastern U.S.

Landscape Form Winter hazel is a spreading, fountainlike deciduous shrub that becomes more densely branched and graceful-looking with age. It is often wider than it is tall, reaching five feet in height and eight feet in width. In spring, the pleated leaves are edged in purple, which fades as the season progresses.

Uses Understory for garden room with tall flowering or shade trees; specimen plant for spring interest

Ornamental Attributes In early spring, shimmering, primrose-yellow flowers held in pendant racemes exude a delicious, sweet fragrance; pale golden fall color adds seasonal interest.

Tolerances Slight to moderate drought, dense shade

Growing Tips Plant winter hazel in a partially shaded spot protected from spring frosts in moist, well-drained acidic soil that has been amended with organic matter. Irrigate it in summer to avoid leaf scald in hot weather. If pruning is necessary, remove the stems all the way to the ground and avoid heading cuts, which encourage an excess of twiggy growth that can spoil the graceful shape of the shrub. The genus is very disease resistant and trouble free.

Cultivars and Related Species *Corylopsis glabrescens* tolerates more sun than other species. It grows to a height of eight feet and brightens the garden with lightly citrus-scented yellow-green blooms from late March until early April. Native to Korea and Japan (Zones 6 to 9), spike winter hazel, *C. spicata,* is more upright in shape and grows to ten feet high and eight feet wide. *C. sinensis,* Chinese winter hazel, is among the tallest species, topping out at 15 feet. Its pendant racemes of buttery-yellow flowers appear later in the spring.

Native Alternative See *Hamamelis,* page 56.

Daphne × burkwoodii | Burkwood Daphne

Native Habitat and Range Hybrid between *Daphne cneorum,* from mountain meadows of southern and central Europe, and *D. caucasica,* native to the Caucasus

Hardiness and Cultivated Range Zones 4 to 9; Northeast, South, Midwest, southern British Columbia, Pacific Northwest to northern California

Landscape Form This very tidy-looking rounded, deciduous to semievergreen shrub quickly reaches four feet in height and width. Its leaves appear as clusters of whorls around the stem, giving the plant a very distinctive look in the garden.

Uses Specimen plant in a courtyard entrance, near a walkway, or next to a terrace where the fragrance can be fully appreciated

Ornamental Attributes Pastel-pink-tinged blooms open in late spring, releasing their legendary heady fragrance; there's often a light rebloom in the fall. The shrub's deep green deciduous to semievergreen foliage is eye-catching.

Tolerances Extreme cold, moderate drought

Growing Tips Plant *Daphne × burkwoodii* in full sun or partial shade in soil enriched with organic matter or humus that's neutral or slightly alkaline. The soil should be well drained and evenly moist but never wet or soggy. Irrigate the shrub in summer and don't allow it

A tidy-looking semievergreen shrub that quickly reaches four feet, Burkwood daphne is a lovely compact specimen plant. Give it a spot near a walkway or terrace so you can enjoy its small fragrant flowers up close.

to dry out. Prune to remove ground-touching branches. Although the genus is notoriously short-lived and many are prone to sudden death, no garden should be *Daphne* deficient.

Cultivars and Related Species *Daphne × burkwoodii* 'Carol Mackie' has deep green leaves edged with a band of light gold

that fades to creamy white in the summer; yellow leaves with green margins characterize 'Briggs Moonlight', a sibling of 'Carol Mackie'; 'Silver Edge' displays green leaves bordered in white, creating a silver-gray effect. *D. caucasica,* native to the Caucasus and western Asia (Zones 6 to 8), is a deciduous species whose white, fragrant flowers are produced throughout the summer. Native to Europe, Turkey, the Caucasus, and Siberia (Zones 4 to 9), *D. mezereum* is winter flowering, with fragrant purple flowers studding the leafless stems. Shiny evergreen leaves rimmed in yellow and clusters of winter-blooming starry purplish-pink flowers distinguish *D. odora* 'Aureomarginata' (Zones 7 to 9).

Native Alternative See *Arctostaphylos denisflora,* manzanita, page 78, and *Myrica gale,* sweet gale (at *Buxus sempervirens,* boxwood), page 81.

Disanthus cercidifolius | Disanthus

Native Habitat and Range Mountains and woodlands of Japan and China

Hardiness and Cultivated Range Zones 5 to 8; Southeast, Pacific Northwest, southwestern British Columbia

Landscape Form This is an upright, rounded shrub ten feet tall and wide with heart-shaped blue-green leaves. Its form becomes more vase-shaped and spreading with maturity.

Uses Autumn interest in woodland garden niche

Ornamental Attributes This plant displays an amazing simultaneous array of fall color: Shades of yellow, red, and dusky purple highlight the garden, falling just as the spidery, slightly fragrant flowers emerge.

Tolerances Frost, dense shade

Growing Tips For best results, select a site in full sun or partial shade protected from strong prevailing winds. Grow this disease- and pest-resistant shrub in moist, well-drained, rich acid soil, and provide summer irrigation, as it resents drying out.

Cultivars and Related Species None.

Native Alternative *Cercis canadensis,* eastern redbud, page 49, is similar in foliage but will grow into a tree unless cut back regularly to keep it shrub-sized.

Enkianthus campanulatus Redvein Enkianthus

Native Habitat and Range Mountains and woodlands of Japan

Hardiness and Cultivated Range Zones 4 to 7; New England, Illinois, British Columbia, south to North Carolina, New Mexico, northern California

Landscape Form This deciduous shrub has an elegant, upright habit when young and becomes more layered, open, and treelike with maturity. It grows 8 to 15 feet tall, depending on the region.

Uses Specimen plant in woodland garden room, shrub border

Ornamental Attributes This deciduous rhododendron relative is an elegant addition to even the smallest garden room. Its mid-green leaves appear almost tufted, clustered at the tips of the branches; in late spring, pendant umbels of creamy-white bells veined with red develop on growth from the previous year. In autumn, the finely textured leaves burst into flaming red, orange, and purple.

Tolerances Clay soil

Left: When combining disanthus with other shrubs in an informal hedge, choose plants that complement the outstanding autumn foliage of this tall vase-shaped shrub.

An elegant addition to a small woodland garden room, redvein enkianthus makes a striking focal point that is illuminated by pretty flower clusters in spring and lit by gorgeous foliage colors in autumn.

Growing Tips Plant this shrub in partial shade or full sun in acidic, moist, fertile, well-drained soil. Provide extra summer water to keep it from drying out. Pruning destroys the beautiful natural form.

Cultivars and Related Species The flowers of *Enkianthus campanulatus* 'Red Bells' are a creamy yellow tipped in crimson; cream-colored urn-shaped bells distinguish f. *albiflorus*. *E. campanulatus* var. *palibinii* is prized for its dark red flowers. Snowy-white flowers and a more compact habit characterize *E. perulatus*, a Japanese native (Zones 6 to 9).

Native Alternatives Native from Alaska south to Wyoming and California

(Zones 4 to 8), *Menziesia ferruginea*, rusty menziesia, is a rangy shrub six to ten feet tall with nodding bells below whorled, rust-red foliage. *M. pilosa*, minniebush, is a delicate version of enkianthus, with small, nodding bells held beneath whorls of hairy, oval foliage. Native to woodlands from New York south to Tennessee and Georgia (Zones 5 to 8), it grows four to six feet tall in rich, acidic soil.

Ericameria nauseosa (*Chrysothamnus nauseosus*) Rubber Rabbitbrush

Native Habitat and Range Desert washes, open hillsides, and high plains from

Alberta, south to Mexico; Great Plains west to British Columbia, California

Hardiness and Cultivated Range Zones 6 to 9; performs best from Great Plains west to California

Landscape Form This upright oval to rounded, small to midsize shrub grows three to four feet tall and wide and has a dense, multistemmed form.

Uses Specimen plant, informal hedge, particularly in arid regions

Ornamental Attributes Glowing yellow asterlike flowers cover this shrub in late summer and autumn, followed by bristly seed clusters. Blue-gray to sea-green long, needlelike deciduous to semievergreen leaves densely clothe the pliable stems.

Tolerances Drought, wind, soil compaction, alkaline soil, moderate air pollution

Growing Tips Plant rubber rabbitbrush in well-drained, poor to average sandy, gravelly, or clay soil with a neutral to alkaline pH in full sun. It grows fairly quickly to three feet and slows with age. It prefers cool summer temperatures; in hot regions, provide afternoon shade. Though this pest-free shrub needs ample water to become established, soggy soil is sure death, as is high humidity.

Cultivars and Related Species This is a variable species with a huge natural range. Two subspecies and numerous varieties are identified in the botanical literature. For gardens, buy from a local source to assure regional adaptability.

Tolerant of drought, reflected heat, and poor soil, Apache plume is a great native plant for a desert garden. It needs vigilant pruning to control its shape and size.

Fallugia paradoxa | Apache Plume

Native Habitat and Range Semidesert foothills in southern California, Arizona, New Mexico, Mexico, Texas

Hardiness and Cultivated Range Zones 6 to 10; Texas, western Oklahoma, Arizona, New Mexico, southern Colorado, southern and central Utah, Nevada, south into Mexico

Landscape Form This upright, twiggy shrub is semievergreen, depending upon the severity of drought conditions. It ranges from four to eight feet in height with a spread of six feet.

Uses Hedge, mass planting in a desert garden

Ornamental Attributes Showy, pristine white flowers resembling single roses bloom in late spring and early summer, followed by feathery plumes that carry and disburse the seeds.

Tolerances Drought, reflected heat, poor soil

Growing Tips Plant Apache plume in full sun to partial shade in unamended soil. Prune it hard to control its size and shape and to keep it from becoming too twiggy.

Cultivars and Related Species *Holodiscus discolor,* ocean spray, another member of the rose family, is native to dry woodlands and forests of western North America (Zones 6 to 9). It is an upright shrub with arching branches to 12 feet tall and wide and plumelike panicles of white flowers that appear in spring. Planted in moist, well-drained soil enriched with humus in sun or partial shade, it is drought tolerant when established.

Fothergilla major (*F. monticola*) Fothergilla, Mountain Witchalder

Native Habitat and Range Forest clearings, rock outcroppings, and roadsides

in the mountains of North Carolina, Tennessee, south to northern Alabama

Hardiness and Cultivated Range Zones 4 to 8; New England, Pacific Northwest, south to Florida, Texas, northern California

Landscape Form This upright oval to rounded shrub grows 6 to 10 feet tall and 4 to 8 feet wide, taking a more open and spreading form with age.

Uses Informal hedge, foundation planting, beneath shade and flowering trees

Ornamental Attributes Mountain witchalder has twiggy zigzag stems bearing fragrant white flowers in early spring; its fall foliage ranges from orange to burgundy.

Tolerances Drought, soil compaction, slight air pollution

Growing Tips Plant witchalder in humus-rich, well-drained acidic soil in full sun (for best foliage color) or partial shade. It is intolerant of limey soils as well as waterlogged conditions. This slow-growing shrub maintains an even, symmetrical shape and seldom needs pruning.

Cultivars and Related Species *Fothergilla major* 'Arkansas Beauty' is rounded and compact (to six feet tall and wide), with good autumn color and tolerance for drought and heat. The excellent-flowering 'Mount Airy' has large oval to rounded, frost-resistant foliage that colors well in late autumn. *Fothergilla gardenii,* a dwarf witchalder native to the Southeast (Zones 5 to 9), is a smaller and less coarsely branched species whose leaves are often narrow with a bluish cast. 'Blue Mist' is valued for its blue-green foliage.

A compact shrub that needs little or no pruning, fothergilla is a great plant for layering. Planted in front of flowering dogwood, it eases the transition from herbaceous plants to trees in this garden.

Place a seat near an oakleaf hydrangea, and visit it often to observe the shrub's large conical flower clusters mature from white in June to pink and finally light brown by late summer. In fall, the rough-textured foliage turns dark maroon.

Plants are less hardy than the species and often exhibit inferior autumn color.

Hydrangea quercifolia | Oakleaf Hydrangea

Native Habitat and Range Forest understory, wooded slopes, and shaded, rocky outcroppings from Georgia to Florida, Mississippi

Hardiness and Cultivated Range Zones 5 to 9; New England, Illinois, British Columbia, south to North Carolina, New Mexico, northern California

Landscape Form This deciduous shrub presents a rounded or mounded outline and grows six to eight feet tall and wide. The leaves, which resemble those of an oak tree, have three to seven lobes and are up to eight inches long. The peeling, papery nutmeg-brown bark adds winter interest.

Uses Mass and foundation planting

Ornamental Attributes Beginning in June, oakleaf hydrangea bears large conical panicles of white sepals and fertile flowers, which become suffused with pink as they mature. In autumn the rough-textured foliage turns the color of aged burgundy wine. The leaves often persist into the winter.

Tolerances More sun and drier soil conditions than other hydrangeas

Growing Tips Oakleaf hydrangea performs best in moist, humus-rich, well-drained soil in full sun (for brightest fall color) to partial shade. Although it

appreciates moisture, it will succumb to root rot if allowed to sit in standing water. Prune it after flowering, as the next season's buds are formed on the previous season's wood.

Cultivars and Related Species *Hydrangea quercifolia* 'Flemygea' (syn. 'Snow Queen') displays its double white florets on pendulous arching panicles over a much longer season than the species. 'Alice' is larger than any of the other *H. quercifolia* cultivars, standing 12 feet tall and wide, with luminous white inflorescences 10 to 14 inches long. 'Pee Wee' and 'Sike's Dwarf' are both new selections that reach three to four feet, great for small garden rooms.

Ilex verticillata | Winterberry

Native Habitat and Range Watershed and wetland areas from Nova Scotia to Minnesota, south to Florida, Arkansas

Hardiness and Cultivated Range Zones 3 to 9; Newfoundland, British Columbia, south to Florida, New Mexico, northern California

Landscape Form This midsize deciduous shrub has an oval-rounded shape with a very twiggy branching structure and glossy dark green leaves two to three inches long. Older plants become leggy and sucker to form colonies, especially if planted in permanently moist soil.

Uses Hedge, mass planting, deciduous screen for pond

Ornamental Attributes The vivid, fire-engine-red berries of *Ilex verticillata* mature in late August and September, contrasting with the green foliage, and persist well into the winter as a food source for birds and wildlife.

Tolerances Moderate drought, wet soil, compacted soil, extreme cold

Growing Tips For best results, plant winterberry in full sun or partial shade in moist, fertile, well-drained acidic soil. If planted in alkaline soil, it is subject to stunted growth and chlorotic foliage. For effective pollination and fruit set, situate one male in close proximity to a group of three to five females.

Cultivars and Related Species At four feet high and wide, *Ilex verticillata* 'Red Sprite' (also sold as 'Nana' or 'Compacta') is the most compact of all the cultivars, with impressive and persistent fruit. 'Aurantiaca' displays golden-orange fruit and is five feet tall and wide. Pollinate both these cultivars with 'Jim Dandy'. Eight feet tall and wide, 'Winter Red' is the best known of this species' cultivars, with dark red berries that hold well into the winter. Use 'Southern Gentleman' as its consort.

Itea virginica | Virginia Sweetspire

Native Habitat and Range Along streams in forest understory from New Jersey to Florida west to Louisiana, Missouri

Hardiness and Cultivated Range Zones 5 to 9; New England, Illinois, British Columbia, south to Florida, New Mexico, northern California

Landscape Form Upright, arching or rounded, deciduous to semievergreen shrub with glistening green leaves up to four inches long.

Uses Semievergreen hedge, understory for blooming or shade trees, focal point in a garden niche

Ornamental Attributes Fall brings a fabulous conflagration of crimson, burgundy,

Left: Persisting into winter, the bright red berries of winterberry, a deciduous holly, keep the shrub looking lively once the foliage has dropped. For effective pollination and fruit set combine one or more female cultivars with a male.

Flowering in early to mid-summer when few other shrubs do, Virginia sweetspire punches up a shrub border and complements summer flowers, such as 'White Sonnet' snapdragon and 'Permanent Wave' rose, pictured here.

and purple leaves that persist well into the winter before dropping. Plants in partial to full shade show autumn color in hues of orange, gold, and scarlet. In early to mid-summer white bottlebrush-like flowers open at a time when few shrubs are blooming.

Tolerances Dry as well as wet soil

Growing Tips Virginia sweetspire prefers full sun to partial shade in moist, acidic soil, but it can adapt to neutral and slightly alkaline soils and either wet or dry situations.

Cultivars and Related Species *Itea virginica* 'Henry's Garnet' is covered with strands of white pearls in early summer and displays rich reddish-purple leaf color in the autumn. 'Little Henry', a new compact sweetspire three feet high and wide, is perfect for planting en masse. When in flower the low, rounded plant is covered in white candles of

bloom; its leaves assume an autumnal glow of garnet and purple. The foliage of another new cultivar, 'Saturnalia', rings of Saturn sweetspire, lights up the fall garden in hues of red, hot-pink, yellow, and orange.

Jamesia americana | Waxflower, Cliffbush

Native Habitat and Range Canyons of pinyon and juniper woodland in mountainous western U.S.

Hardiness and Cultivated Range Zones 3 to 8; Rockies of southern Canada, south to New Mexico, west to British Columbia, California

Landscape Form This midsize, upright, bushy deciduous shrub grows to six feet and has rough-textured foliage.

Uses Rock garden, hedge, foundation planting

Ornamental Attributes Fragrant waxy, five-petaled, star-shaped white flowers appear in terminal panicles in late spring and early summer. The bright green foliage transforms to brilliant red, orange, and pink with the onset of fall. Flaking cinnamon-colored bark is noticeable in the winter.

Tolerances Drought, when established

Growing Tips For the best autumn color, site waxflower in full sun in well-drained loam or gravelly soil of average fertility. Provide supplemental water until it is established. After flowering, prune the old canes to the ground to maintain good branching structure.

Cultivars and Related Species *Jamesia americana* is a genus of one species but is closely related to the genus *Deutzia*, native to Asia and Central America. *D. crenata* 'Nikko' (Zones 5 to 8) is a graceful groundcover two feet tall spreading to four feet, with pristine white flowers in late spring and vibrant burgundy foliage in the fall. Although it is an old cultivar, introduced in 1925, the bright pink and white flowers of 'Magician' (Zones 5 to 9) still delight American gardeners.

Leucophyllum frutescens
Silverleaf, Texas Barometer Bush, Texas Ranger, Texas Sage

Native Habitat and Range Semidesert areas of southwestern U.S., Mexico

Hardiness and Cultivated Range Zones 8 to 9; Colorado, Texas, New Mexico, Arizona

Landscape Form This arching, rounded, compact shrub grows to five high and eight feet wide with a luminous silhouette.

To show off the shimmering stems and silver-gray leaves of the aptly named silverleaf, plant the compact shrub next to plants with contrasting shades of foliage.

Uses Mass and foundation planting, rock garden, desert garden, hedge

Ornamental Attributes Shimmering silver stems and silver-gray leaves overlaid with white hairs add a ghostly effect to the landscape. Small lavender-purple flowers, borne in the leaf axils, appear after rainfall.

Tolerances Heat, drought, salt

Growing Tips Site silverleaf in full sun in well-draining sandy loam in a sheltered location. Provide supplemental water only until it's established—too much water and fertilizer can cause ranginess over time. It withstands hard pruning to control its size and shape.

Cultivars and Related Species 'Silverado Sage',a new cultivar of *Leucophyllum frutescens*, is denser and more compact than the species, growing to four by four feet. 'Compactum' is more upright and open than 'Silverado Sage' and makes a good hedge. 'Green Cloud' has lavender-pink flowers and greener leaves.

The small leaves and fine texture of boxleaf honeysuckle lend themselves to pruning and shaping, making this a versatile shrub in many situations. The cultivar 'Baggesen's Gold', shown here, requires a partially shady spot, which works nicely to show off its chartreuse-colored evergreen foliage.

Lonicera nitida | Boxleaf Honeysuckle

Native Habitat and Range Woodland understory of southwestern China

Hardiness and Cultivated Range Zones 6 to 9; southeastern U.S., southern British Columbia, Pacific Northwest, south to California

Landscape Form Left untended, this dense, bushy, low-growing, arching evergreen shrub spreads ten feet wide and tall. Tiny dark green glossy leaves arranged in pairs along the stem create a fine textural affect.

Uses Hedge, topiary, specimen plant

Ornamental Attributes The small leaves and refined texture of boxleaf honeysuckle lend themselves to pruning and shaping. The insignificant flowers are followed by royal-purple berries.

Tolerances Heavy clay soils

Growing Tips Boxleaf honeysuckle per-forms best in moist, well-drained fertile, neutral soil in sun or partial shade. Prune or shear to shape in midsummer and regularly clean out interior deadwood.

Cultivars and Related Species With its long, arching stems sheathed in chartreuse-yellow leaves, *Lonicera nitida* 'Baggesen's Gold' is a shining star in the garden. Plant it in partial shade, since it fades and burns in full sun. Claret-red new growth enhances the appeal of 'Red Tips', a newer cultivar. The green leaves edged in creamy white of 'Silver Frost' read as silver in the garden. 'Lemon Beauty' has dark, inky-green leaves gilded with lemon and lime.

Native Alternative *Paxistima myrsinites*, Oregon boxwood, is a rounded evergreen shrub to three feet tall with deep green, opposite leaves on stiff stems, native to dense western woods from Alberta south to Mexico (Zones 5 to 9).

In a shady garden room, Oregon grape provides shiny leaf color year-round. New foliage on this short-statured shrub emerges tinged with bronze-red, and in fall and winter the leaves have a purplish hue.

Mahonia aquifolium
Oregon Grape

Native Habitat and Range Open, often dry and rocky slopes and forests from southern British Columbia to northern California, northern Idaho

Hardiness and Cultivated Range Zones 5 to 9; New England, Illinois, British Columbia, south to Georgia, New Mexico, northern California

Landscape Form This upright, suckering, clump-forming evergreen shrub grows six feet high and wide. It has pinnate leaves composed of leaflets resembling holly leaves and offers striking, year-round interest.

Uses Hedge or hedgerow; beneath shade and flowering trees

Ornamental Attributes New growth is tinged with bronze-red, and in the autumn and winter the foliage assumes hints of reddish purple. Displays of electric yellow flowers in erect racemes in late winter are followed by abundant edible purple-blue fruits in autumn. The fruits look like small grapes and are very attractive to birds.

Tolerances Dry soil, dense shade, root competition, acidic soil, salt

Growing Tips Grow Oregon grape in moist, well-drained soil rich in humus in full or partial shade. Provide supplemental water until the plant is established. Prune to remove unwanted suckers. Mahonias require pollination by the same or a compatible species.

Cultivars and Related Species *Mahonia aquifolium* 'Compactum', a good ground-cover for sites with root competition,

reaches two feet high and three feet wide and has good russet-bronze winter color. Native to the Cascades (Zones 6 to 8), *M. nervosa* is a dwarf that spreads by suckering. *M. fremontii,* desert mahonia, comes from Mexico and the southwestern U.S. (Zones 8 to 11). It has an open branching habit with sharply toothed glaucous leaflets and reaches six feet tall and wide. *Mahonia × media* 'Charity' is a vigorous, upright shrub with stunning architectural presence. Its canary-yellow flowers exude a delicate fragrance that attracts hummingbirds and bees. It grows six feet tall and is hardy in Zones 7 to 10.

Osmanthus fragrans | Fragrant Olive, Sweet olive

Native Habitat and Range Woodland and forest understory in China, Japan, the Himalaya

Hardiness and Cultivated Range Zones 8 to 11; coastal Virginia, Pacific Northwest, Southeast

From fall to early spring, fragrant olive produces many small flowers that give off a heady perfume. Be sure to plant this very large shrub where you can appreciate its sweet apricot scent as you walk by.

Landscape Form This vigorous, upright, large evergreen shrub has dark green leaves four to five inches long with a finely serrated edge. It attains a height and width of 20 feet, becoming leggier as it ages.

Uses Foundation planting, hedge, espalier, specimen plant, screen, container plant

Ornamental Attributes Small, bright white, tubular flowers held in clusters are abundant in autumn, winter, and early spring and may sporadically appear during the summer. Although the flowers are small, they give off a very heady sweet apricot fragrance; they've been used for centuries in China to make an aromatic tea.

Tolerances Heavy clay soil, acidic soil, moderate salt

Growing Tips Plant fragrant olive in moist, fertile, well-drained neutral to acid soil. It thrives in high shade but can grow in full sun with protection from hot afternoon sun and strong winds. It

is very disease and pest resistant. Prune to maintain size, shape, and to promote a strong branching structure.

Cultivars and Related Species Orange flowers and dark green smooth-edged leaves characterize *Osmanthus fragrans* f. *aurantiacus.* 'Conger Yellow' has tiny butter-yellow flowers with the same tantalizing fragrance and growth habit as the species. Native to Japan and Taiwan (Zones 7 to 9), *O. heterophyllus* is an evergreen shrub 12 inches tall and wide. It has glossy dark green leaves that are opposite and smooth, and its highly scented clusters of white flowers bloom in fall. 'Goshiki', a compact and slow-growing cultivar six to eight feet tall and wide, displays green hollylike foliage overlaid with pink, orange, yellow, and cream.

Native Alternative *Osmanthus americanus,* devilwood, is a large shrub to small tree with an open form and elongated semievergreen leaves and fragrant but inconspicuous flowers borne in summer. It is hardy in Zones 7 to 10.

Rhapidophyllum hystrix | Needle Palm, Porcupine Palm

Native Habitat and Range Wooded, swampy areas from southern South Carolina to central Florida, west to southern Mississippi

Hardiness and Cultivated Range Zones 7 to 10; Southeast west to Texas, southern British Columbia, south to California

Landscape Form This small, clump-forming trunkless palm is distinguished by short branches that begin at ground level. Each leaf stalk produces a deeply

For a bit of drama in the garden, give needle palm a prominent spot where the architecture of this unusually shaped trunkless palm can be fully appreciated.

lobed leaf that is bright green tinged with blue-green on the underside. Fiberlike sheaths at the base of the plant bear short needles. It reaches 5 to 6 feet in height and 6 to 12 feet in width.

Uses Specimen plant, foundation planting, container plant

Ornamental Attributes The deep green, fan-shaped foliage and rounded habit of needle palms add drama in the garden.

Tolerances Purportedly the most cold tolerant of all the palms; heat

Growing Tips Plant the needle palm in moderately fertile, moist but very well drained soil in partial shade or sun. In full sun the crown becomes congested and compacted and the leaves loose their luster.

Cultivars and Related Species The cabbage palm, *Sabal palmetto,* also from the southern U.S. (Zones 8 to 12), forms a twisted crown atop a single, nonbranching trunk

that reaches 50 to 60 feet. *Sabal minor,* blue-stem or bush palmetto, is a rounded, compact fan palm with a trunk that stays below ground. The leaves vary in length and width from one to five feet, and the creamy flowers stand above the foliage in arching panicles. It is native to moist forests and bottomlands from North Carolina to Texas (Zones 7, with protection, to 10). If killed to the ground it often comes back from the root. *Trachycarpus fortunei,* the Chinese windmill palm, from central and eastern China (Zones 8 to 11) is very cold tolerant. Its dark green fan-shaped fronds radiate out from the trunk, which rises to 30 feet.

Ribes sanguineum | Red-Flowering Currant, Winter Currant

Native Habitat and Range Low and middle elevations of shady woods and forests to open and rocky sites from southern

British Columbia to northern California from the Cascades to the Coast Range

Hardiness and Cultivated Range Zones 6 to 10; southern British Columbia, Pacific Northwest, northern California, Southeast

Landscape Form This deciduous shrub reaching six to ten feet tall and wide has upright, graceful stems and dark green lobed leaves.

Uses Specimen plant, informal hedge or hedgerow

Ornamental Attributes Drooping racemes of rosy-pink flowers decorate the stems in spring, inviting hummingbirds to feast. Other birds are drawn to the spherical blue fruits in fall and winter.

Tolerances Moderate drought

Growing Tips Site currants in full sun in humus-rich, moderately fertile well-drained soil, and provide supplemental water until they are established. Thin congested plants by pruning back a third of the oldest growth at ground level after the bloom season ends. This shrub may partially or fully defoliate in summer.

Cultivars and Related Species *Ribes sanguineum* 'Brocklebankii' electrifies the garden with gleaming yellow foliage and soft pink flowers. Placed in partial shade to avoid leaf scorch, it slowly grows five to six feet tall and wide. 'White Icicle' cools down the garden with elegant drooping clusters of snowy blooms juxtaposed against the new, bright green foliage. The vivid crimson-pink flowers of 'King Edward VII' are the brightest of all the cultivars. *Ribes speciosum,* the fuchsia-flowered currant, is native to Oregon and California (Zones 7 to 10).

Left: The large flowers of lenten rose draw attention to the delicate drooping flower clusters of 'White Icicle' flowering currant.
Right: Yellow elder flowers from late winter through summer in intermittent flushes.

Shiny foliage, blood-red flowers with long stamens, and thorny stems make this 10- to 12-foot shrub a garden standout. Native to the Midwest (Zones 5 to 9), the buffalo currant, *Ribes odoratum,* has yellow flowers with a sweet, spicy fragrance followed by edible black fruit.

Tecoma stans | Yellow Elder, Trumpetbush, Yellowbells

Native Habitat and Range Dry forests and desert shrublands from Texas and Arizona through Central and South America

Hardiness and Cultivated Range Zones 10 to 12; Texas, Arizona, Florida

Landscape Form This densely branched evergreen shrub or multitrunked small tree grows 15 to 25 feet tall and up to 15 feet high. Its bright green foliage is pinnate with long oval leaflets resembling *Sambucus nigra* subsp. *canadensis.*

Uses Specimen plant, screen, hedge, container plant

Ornamental Attributes Pendant funnel-shaped, sunshine-yellow flowers are produced in clusters at the branch tips from late winter through summer in intermittent flushes, giving rise to interesting seedpods shaped like string beans.

Tolerances Sandy soil, alkaline conditions

Growing Tips Plant yellow elder in moist, well-drained, fertile soil in full sun sheltered from strong wind. It tolerates a wide range of soil conditions and may be cut to the ground in early spring to rejuvenate or sheared to control size and shape and promote rebloom.

Cultivars and Related Species *Tecoma capensis* may be grown as a shrub or a climber. As a climber it can scramble 20 feet. Orange to scarlet tubular flowers provide summer interest on this South African native, which is best grown in tropical and subtropical areas, as it suffers below 32°F. 'Apricot' is compact, growing to five feet tall and three feet wide, with bright flowers of apricot-orange; 'Lutea', a slow grower to six feet, has dark yellow flowers.

Viburnum prunifolium | Black Haw, Stagbrush

Native Habitat and Range Open forest clearings and understory from Michigan, Northeast, south to Texas, Florida

Hardiness and Cultivated Range Zones 3 to 9; Midwest, Northeast, Southeast, Pacific Northwest

Landscape Form Black haw forms either a large shrub 15 feet tall and 10 feet wide or a small tree with a rounded canopy. It

Depending on your preferences, black haw can be trained as a small tree with an open rounded canopy, as shown here, or as a large shrub with multiple stems.

is deciduous, with shiny, dark green ovate leaves.

Uses Specimen plant, hedgerow

Ornamental Attributes Flattened cymes of white flowers two to four inches wide appear in April and May. Fall color is subtle but noticeable with leaves suffused with red and purple and edible navy-blue fruits that attract birds.

Tolerances Drought

Growing Tips Site black haw in full sun or partial shade in moderately fertile, well-drained soil. It is very adaptable but doesn't like perpetually wet feet, and the foliage is susceptible to powdery mildew. Older, congested plants can be rejuvenated by removing a third of the old stems at ground level after flowering.

Cultivars and Related Species *Viburnum* × *bodnantense* 'Dawn' is upright and slightly vase-shaped, with highly scented tubular pink flowers borne in clusters on bare branches in late winter and early

Limbed up and grown as a small tree, this chaste tree perfectly complements the scale of the house, softening the strong horizontal lines and adding just the right amount of height to the facade. Its shape beautifully echoes the forms of the smaller shrubs planted close to the wall.

spring and red fall color. It is hardy in Zones 5 to 8. Spicy fragrance pervades the garden when *Viburnum carlesii,* Koreanspice viburnum, presents its domed heads of waxy white flowers. Red berries appear in autumn paired with burgundy-colored foliage. It reaches eight feet at maturity and is hardy in Zones 4 to 8. *Viburnum tinus,* native to the Mediterranean region (Zones 7 to 9), is a compact evergreen shrub with fragrant white flowers displayed against a background of deep green, shiny leaves in late winter and spring. It is suitable for sun or partial shade and does well in coastal areas. 'Variegatum' has yellow-margined leaves.

Vitex agnus-castus | Chaste Tree, Monk's Pepper

Native Habitat and Range Woodlands and dry riverbeds in the Mediterranean, southern China

Hardiness and Cultivated Range Zones 6 to 9; Maryland to southern U.S, west to Texas, New Mexico, Washington to California

Landscape Form This deciduous shrub or small tree has a rounded, broad habit and spreading crown. The aromatic gray-green leaves are composed of five to seven leaflets, creating a hazy, delicate texture. Although it may die back in northern areas, it comes back from the root. It grows rapidly to 15 to 25 feet tall and wide.

Uses Specimen plant, container plant

Ornamental Attributes The spectacular fluorescent blue-purple terminal flower spikes that cover the plant during the summer make it easily mistaken for a *Buddleja*. Hummingbirds and bees frequent the blooms. Older plants have lovely tan-gray, scaly bark.

Tolerances Drought, salt

Growing Tips Plant chaste tree in full sun in well-drained, moist, moderately fertile soil. It grows faster and produces more flowers with light applications of fertilizer and mulch. Prune in winter, as the plant flowers on new wood; it may be cut to the ground annually in northern regions.

Cultivars and Related Species *Vitex agnus-castus* 'Shoal Creek' becomes a small tree with gray-green foliage and violet flower spikes from June through September. It is very heat tolerant and performs well in southern and western regions. *Vitex trifolia* 'Purpurea', Arabian lilac, an open spreading shrub with clusters of small purple flowers and interesting woolly leaves tinged with purple, is a choice plant for dry or drought-prone climates and naturalistic gardens.

Native Alternative Native to open woods and clearings in the Southeast (Zones 4 to 8), *Aesculus parviflora,* bottlebrush buckeye, has fragrant wands of white summer flowers above opposite, palmately divided leaves and clear yellow autumn color.

Yucca filamentosa | Adam's Needle

Native Habitat and Range Sandy dry rock outcroppings, open woods, and fields in Southeast, west to Tennessee, Mississippi

Hardiness and Cultivated Range Zones 4 to 10; Nova Scotia, British Columbia, south to Georgia, New Mexico, California

Landscape Form This clump-forming evergreen shrub is usually trunkless, with basal leaves forming large rosettes five feet tall and wide. Its stiff, straplike blue-green leaves are an inch wide and two to three feet long. The leaf margins peel off in thin threads or filaments.

Uses Mass planting or specimen plant in rock garden or desertscape, container plant

Ornamental Attributes Flower stalks rise six to ten feet, displaying dozens of nodding, waxy white bells that may be flushed with cream or palest green in mid- and late summer.

Tolerances Drought, heat, poor soil, salt

Growing Tips Adam's needle prefers full sun in well-drained loamy soil, though it can tolerate light shade and sandy soil. Be wary of the sharp leaves when working around them in the garden.

Cultivars and Related Species *Yucca filamentosa* 'Color Guard' is hard to ignore: The center of each bright green leaf is striped in electrifying yellow-gold. It grows in yard-wide clumps with six-foot bloom stalks in late spring. 'Golden Sword' has gleaming yellow foliage edged in dark green and exhibits a looser, less rigid habit. *Yucca rostrata,* beaked blue yucca, is native to Texas and Mexico (Zones 5 to 10)and has silver-blue leaves radiating out from a central stalk that can reach ten feet tall.

Left: The bright green rounded pads of low-growing prickly pear set off the tall blue-green spikes of Adam's needle.

Perennials

Acanthus hungaricus, A. mollis, bear's breeches

Achillea species and hybrids, yarrow

Aconitum carmichaelii, monkshood

Agapanthus species and hybrids, lily-of-the-Nile

Agastache rupestris, licorice mint, sunset hyssop

Agave havardiana, A. parryi, century plant

Amsonia species, bluestar

Arisaema heterophyllum, dancing crane cobra lily

Aruncus dioicus, goatsbeard

Asphodeline aestivus, Turkish asphodel

Aster species and cultivars, aster

Athyrium filix-femina, tatting fern

Baptisia australis, wild indigo

Calamagrostis × *aucutiflora* and *C. brachytricha,* feather reed grass

Canna × *generalis,* canna lily, Indian shot

Carex pendula, drooping sedge, hanging sedge

Castilleja species, Indian paintbrush

Dalea purpurea, purple prairie clover

Dasilirion wheeleri, desert spoon, sotol

Delphinium species and hybrids, delphinium

Dryopteris erythrosora, autumn fern

Echinacea species and hybrids, coneflower

Echinops ritro, globe thistle

Eriogonum umbellatum, sulfur buckwheat

Eryngium amethystinum, amethyst sea holly

Eupatorium purpureum, joe-pye weed

Euphorbia species, spurge

Hakonechloa macra 'Aureola', hakone grass, Japanese forest grass

Hedychium coronarium, butterfly ginger

Helianthus species, sunflower

Hemerocallis species and hybrids, daylily

Hesperaloe parviflora, red yucca

Hibiscus coccineus, scarlet mallow

Iris ensata 'Variegata', striped Japanese iris

Kniphofia species and hybrids, red hot poker

Lespedeza thunbergii, Thunberg bushclover

Liatris spicata, gayfeather

Ligularia tussilaginea 'Crispata' and cultivars, leopard plant

Macleaya cordata, plume poppy

Molinia caerulea, purple moor grass

Monarda didyma and hybrids, bee balm

Once the trees and shrubs that form its bones are in place, the garden can be fleshed out with colorful, fragrant perennials and annuals. These plants entice butterflies and hummingbirds near your seat, and postbloom seedpods can provide food for birds and visual interest throughout the winter months.

Morina longifolia, whorlflower

Muhlenbergia dumosa, bamboo muhly

Nolina parryi, bear grass

Opuntia species, prickly pear cactus

Paeonia species and hybrids, peony

Panicum virgatum, switchgrass

Patrinia scabiosifolia, golden lace

Penstemon species and hybrids, pentstemon

Perovskia atriplicifolia, Russian sage

Phlomis fruticosa, Jerusalem sage

Plumbago auriculata, Cape leadwort

Polystichum munitum, western sword fern

Ratibida columnifera, Mexican hat

Rodgersia pinnata, rodgersia

Romneya coulteri, Matilija poppy, tree poppy

Rudbeckia nitida 'Herbstsonne', autumn sun coneflower

Ruellia brittoniana, common ruellia

Saccharum ravennae, ravenna grass, hardy pampas grass

Salvia greggii, autumn sage, cherry sage

Salvia guaranitica, Brazilian sage, blue anise sage

Salvia nemerosa, meadow sage

Salvia officinalis, culinary sage

Silphium laciniatum, compass plant

Silphium perfoliatum, cup plant

Solidago rugosa, goldenrod

Stipa gigantea, giant feather reed grass, golden oats

Thalictrum species, meadow rue

Veratrum viride, false hellebore

Veronicastrum virginicum, Culver's root

Vines

Actinidia kolomikta, Kolomikta kiwi

Aristolochia macrophylla, Dutchman's pipe

Aster carolinianus, climbing aster

Bignonia capreolata, cross vine

Billardiera longiflora, billardiera

Campsis grandiflora, *C. radicans,* trumpetvine

Celastrus scandens, American bittersweet

Clematis species and hybrids, clematis

Cobaea scandens, cup and saucer vine

Decumaria barbara, climbing hydrangea

Dicentra scandens, bleeding heart vine

Distictis buccinatoria, blood-red trumpet

Ficus pumila, creeping fig

Gelsemium sempervirens, Carolina jessamine

Holboellia coriacea, holboellia

Hydrangea anomala, climbing hydrangea

Hydrangea seemannii, hydrangea vine

Ipomoea species, morning glory

Jasminum polyanthum, jasmine

Kadsura japonica, scarlet kadsura

Lablab purpureus, hyacinth bean

Lathyrus latifolius, perennial sweet pea

Lonicera × heckrotii, goldflame honeysuckle

Lonicera sempervirens, trumpet honeysuckle

Parthenocissus quinquefolia, woodbine

Parthenocissus tricuspidata, Boston ivy

Passiflora species, passion vine

Plumbago auriculata, Cape plumbago

Rosa banksiae, Lady Banks rose

Schisandra chinensis, Chinese schisandra

Schizophragma hydrangeoides, Japanese hydrangea vine

Smilax walteri, coral greenbriar

Solanum crispum 'Glasnevin', potato vine

Stauntonia hexaphylla, stauntonia

Tecoma capensis, Cape honeysuckle

Thunbergia alata, black-eyed Susan vine

Trachyspermum jasminoides, star jasmine

Vitis vinifera, grape

Wisteria frutescens, American wisteria

Left: Climbers such as this Japanese hydrangea vine can bring color and texture to an otherwise dull blank wall. They also help create strong vertical structure in a garden room.

Groundcovers

Arctostaphylos uva-ursi, bearberry

Ardisia japonica, marlberry

Asarum canadense, A. arifolium, wild ginger

Bergenia cordifolia, bergenia

Calluna vulgaris, heather

Campanula poscharskyana, Serbian bellflower

Carex pensylvanica, Pennsylvania sedge

Ceratostigma species, leadplant

Dryopteris × *australis,* Dixie woodfern

Epimedium species, barrenwort

Galium odoratum, sweet woodruff

Gaultheria procumbens, wintergreen

Gaultheria shallon, Salal

Geranium macrorrhizum, bigroot geranium

Helianthemum nummularium, rock rose

Helleborus × *hybridus,* Lenten rose

Heuchera 'Pewter Veil', coral bells

Hosta species and cultivars, hosta

Juniperus horizontalis, creeping juniper

Liriope muscari, lily-turf

Lysimachia nummularia 'Aurea', moneywort

Mahonia repens, creeping mahonia

Matteuccia struthiopteris, ostrich fern

Microbiota decussata, Russian arborvitae

Omphalodes cappadocica, navel seed

Ophiopogon planiscapus, mondo grass

Paxistima myrsinites, Oregon boxwood

Phlomis russeliana, Jerusalem sage

Phlox subulata, moss phlox

Photinia davidiana 'Prostrata'

Plumbago auriculata, Cape plumbago

Rhus aromatica 'Grow Low', fragrant sumac

Ruscus aculeatus, butcher's broom

Sarcococca hookeriana var. *humilis,*
  S. ruscifolia, sweet box

Saxifraga × *urbium,* London pride

Sedum species, stonecrop

Stachys byzantina, lamb's ear

Thymus species, thyme

Tiarella cordifolia, foamflower

Vaccinium crassifolium, creeping blueberry

Vancouveria hexandra, inside-out flower

Veronica prostrata, creeping speedwell

Viburnum davidii, David viburnum

Right: The small scale of groundcovers lends an air of intimacy to the garden room. Shade-loving species can fill spaces beneath trees and shrubs, and aromatic plants, as shown here, encourage lingering.

USDA Hardiness Zone Map

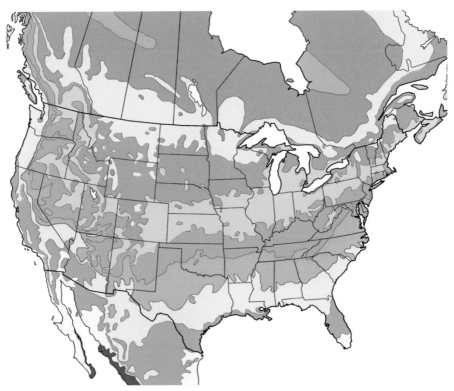

Zones and Minimum Winter Temperatures (°F.)

Zone 1 below −50°

Zone 2 −50° to −40°

Zone 3 −40° to −30°

Zone 4 −30° to −20°

Zone 5 −20° to 10°

Zone 6 −10° to 0°

Zone 7 0° to 10°

Zone 8 10° to 20°

Zone 9 20° to 30°

Zone 10 30° to 40°

Zone 11 above 40°

Contributors

C. Colston Burrell is a garden designer, photographer, naturalist, and award-winning author. A certified chlorophyll addict, Cole is an avid and lifelong plantsman, gardener, and birdwatcher. He gardens on ten acres in the Blue Ridge Mountains near Charlottesville, Virginia, and is principal of Native Landscape Design and Restoration, which specializes in blending nature and culture through artistic design. Cole has published several books on gardening and writes regularly for such publications as *Fine Gardening, Horticulture, Landscape Architecture,* and *American Gardener.* He has edited or contributed to 13 BBG handbooks, including most recently *Spring-Blooming Bulbs* (2002), *The Sunny Border* (2002), and *Summer-Blooming Bulbs* (2001).

Lucy Hardiman was to the garden born. Most of the childhood memories of this fifth-generation Oregon gardener revolve around the cycles and seasons in the garden. Lucy's urban garden has been featured in numerous publications and is a frequent tour destination. A popular lecturer, teacher, and author, Lucy is a contributing editor for *Horticulture* magazine and pens a column for *Northwest Garden News;* she also writes for *Fine Gardening, Dig,* and *Pacific Horticulture.* She is past president of the Hardy Plant Society of Oregon.

Illustrations

Paul Harwood

Photos

Karen Bussolini cover, pages 2, 4, 8, 10, 22, 24, 27, 28, 29, 38, 40, 44, 47, 54, 57, 91, 113

Jerry Pavia pages 6, 14, 15, 19, 20 (Holzknecht garden, designed by Freeland & Sabrina Tanner), 43, 46, 49, 52, 59, 67, 69, 76, 78, 79, 85, 88, 90, 94, 96, 102, 110

Lucy Hardiman pages 7, 12, 13, 39

David Cavagnaro pages 9, 36, 45, 48, 58, 63, 65, 74, 83, 84, 86, 87, 93, 99, 104

C. Colston Burrell pages 16, 26

Christine Douglas pages 17, 50, 61, 62, 73, 97, 101, 105

Alan & Linda Detrick pages 21, 53, 56, 60, 92, 109

Neil Soderstrom page 25

Derek Fell pages 51, 55, 68, 81, 82, 98, 103, 106

Charles Marden Fitch pages 64, 70, 72, 100

Walter Chandoha page 80

Index

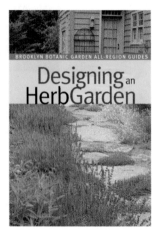

More Information on Intimate Gardens

Designing an Herb Garden has everything you need to create a dazzling herb garden—simple garden plans, plant recommendations, and indispensable growing tips. For more inspiring designs and practical gardening advice, check out these BBG handbooks: *Pruning Trees, Shrubs & Vines, The Potted Garden, Japanese-Inspired Gardens,* and *The Natural Water Garden.*

Ordering Books From Brooklyn Botanic Garden

World renowned for pioneering gardening information, Brooklyn Botanic Garden's award-winning guides provide practical advice for gardeners in every region of North America.

Join Brooklyn Botanic Garden as an annual Subscriber Member and receive three gardening handbooks, delivered directly to you, each year. Other benefits include free admission to many public gardens across the country, plus three issues of *Plants & Gardens News, Members News,* and our guide to courses and public programs.

For additional information on Brooklyn Botanic Garden, including other membership packages, call 718-623-7210 or visit our website at www.bbg.org. To order other fine titles published by BBG, call 718-623-7286 or shop in our online store at www.bbg.org/gardengiftshop.